BUCHLYVIE

A VILLAGE IN STIRLINGSHIRE

J.R. BUREAU

Buchlyvie from East.

View of Buchlyvie from the East

© J. R. Bureau.
1996

Cover Illustration by
Christine Thomson

Published by
Stirling Library Services

ISBN 1 870 542 33 9

Printed by
Cordfall Ltd, Glasgow
0141 332 4640

ACKNOWLEDGEMENTS

Many of the villagers of Buchlyvie, having heard rumours of the writing of this book, showed immediate interest in helping to bring it to fruition. To them should go our first thanks. Some of them gave more than average, in the form of notes on a variety of subjects, sight of their treasured historical possessions and sometimes just their memories:

Etta Bennie, George Bennie, Cecily Bentley, Walter Bilsland, Alec Buchanan, Jeanie Buchanan, Mary Bruce, Catriona Cowan, Ian Drysdale, Andrew Dun, Maragaret Dun, Agnes Forrester, Billy Gordon, Edward Harrison, Nick Holding,Isobel McAllion, Margaret McCallum, Jock McGreggor, John McKay, Jennifer McLellan, Betty McEwan, Betty Martin, Willie Martin, Forrester Millar, Bobby Morrison, Jean Morrison, David Muirhead, Elspeth Murdoch, Gina O'Brien, Ena Oldham, Fr.Seamus Rehill, Doris Retson, Eleanor Risk, John Risk, Christine Ritchie, Jessie Ritchie, Cora Ross, Duncan Ross, Angus Stewart, Andrew J. Stewart, Jean Stewart, Fiona Stirling, James Stirling.

We owe a particular debt to the Stirling Archivist, George A.Dixon, who furnished a lot of the historical material, and guided us to much more. We also owe a great debt to the *Stirling Observer* as a major source of information, and to the late Alex Weir who was one of their Buchlyvie correspondents for so many years.

A great deal of the core research and general winkling–out of local information was in the hands of Cora Ross and Janey Fleming.The latter, as Chairman of the Community Council, was also burdened with the overall responsibility of bringing the book into being.

We have the great good fortune of having a professional artist in the community, Christine Thomson, who was happy to be commissioned to undertake some of the drawings of the village – including those on the front and back covers. Hardly less professional are the smaller sketches which Frank Ellen did for us of – for example the school, Auchentroig and Garden. Also, Billy Pretorious did the delightful cartoons in the book.

We took an early decision that Buchlyvie people, particularly of the last 150 years, should be the main centre of interest in the book. While this is easily managed through photographs, it is harder to include lists of people in the text without becoming over–detailed and ultimately very boring. We hit on the solution of listing all the names we had come across in our researches and putting them at the back of the book. If we have left out anyone who should be there, we apologise.

We must finally thank Stirling Council Libraries for their financial support in this venture, and Local History Officer, Elma Lindsay.

The book had to be written in unexpected haste. That is my excuse for any serious failure in its writing. Yet, in spite of the urgency, I have found writing it immensely enjoyable.

Jack Bureau,
The Bank House,
Buchlyvie
18 May 1996

CONTENTS

Aerial view of Buchlyvie

I
INTRODUCTION

In the narrow waist of central Scotland, between the Highland mountains to the north and the gentler hills of the Lowlands to the south, it takes only about an hour to drive from the Atlantic Ocean to the North Sea.

From Dumbarton on the Firth of Clyde, an eighteenth century British Army disembarking to quell the latest rebellious uprising in support of the Stuarts, could march along that same road to Stirling, a distance of about thirty miles as the crow flies, and from there board a boat and sail down the Forth on a favourable tide, past Edinburgh and out into the North Sea

On its way to Stirling, such an army would have had to march through a number of small villages that lay along the road: Gartocharn, Drymen, Buchlyvie and

Arnprior, Kippen, Gargunnock and Cambusbarron, before arriving at the Royal Burgh of Stirling, dominated by its castle.

At some of these villages no doubt a halt would have been called for rest and refreshment, and some tests made of the local ales. Buchlyvie would certainly have been a stopping point, for there would still be nearly fifteen miles to march before arriving at Stirling.

As the troops marched along the curve of the military road as it arches north from Dumbarton and sweeps east to Stirling, they would have been increasingly aware of the startling beauty of the countryside. Marching the last few miles before reaching Buchlyvie, they would have seen on their left the great panorama of the Breadalbane mountains, the southernmost boundary of

The Village from the West (Frank Ellen)

The Moss Water Wheel – 1768

Lord Kames's Water Wheel (Frank Ellen, after K. Mackay)

the Highlands of Scotland: from Ben Lomond overlooking Loch Lomond, east across the ancient volcanic peaks of Ben Venue and Ben Ledi and Ben Vorlich in the distance down to the Hills of Menteith and the wooded fastness of Rob Roy MacGregor's country around the Trossachs, which can be seen north, straight across the valley from Buchlyvie village.

The mountains were a constant reminder to the villagers of the potential threat from the turbulent Highlanders who, partly from a tradition of tribal belligerence, and partly from a history of inescapable and constant poverty, were apt to come down from their meagre homes to confiscate the lowlanders' cattle, fattening in the meadows of the fertile land below.

The Carse of Stirling – the three to four miles of flat land which lies between these mountains and the road on which the soldiers were marching, consisted then largely of bog, marsh and 'moss', deep blankets of peat, covering fertile clays, which were to provide reforming landowners in the eighteenth century with great opportunities for new wealth through land improvement: Flanders Moss, Cardross Moss, Blairdrummond Moss, Drip Moss.

On the opposite side of the road, these troops would have seen grasslands sloping steadily up six hundred feet to the rough pastures of the moors, above and to the south of the village, where the sheep and

the cattle grazed. In those days Ballindalloch Muir, Balgair Muir, Buchlyvie Muir and Kippen Muir gave steady grazing to large herds and flocks, both to local animals and those brought down from the Highlands to be fattened, sold and driven down to English markets, following the union of the royal dynasties in 1603. Drovers going directly due south from Buchlyvie would have taken the cattle through the passes of the Fintry Hills and the Campsie Fells before driving the beasts down to Glasgow (population: 32, 000) on the River Clyde.

In the eighteenth century, the village was heavily involved in the religious fervour concerning what they felt was the Church of Scotland's failure to uphold the principles of the Covenant. Perhaps the biggest event in the village (if we ignore the terrors of the plague which threatened it regularly from 1349 up to the middle of 17th century, and the horror and destruction of famine every time there were serious crop failures) was the building of the North Church on the Aberfoyle road, associated with the 1733 Secession movement in the Scottish Kirk.

In the nineteenth century, working and living conditions in the village, still appalling by modern standards, improved everywhere, as greater productivity and competence in trade, industry and in agriculture lead to an improvement of living standards. As the village moved towards the end of the nineteenth century there was enough wealth locally to justify the building of a branch of the Bank of Scotland at the top of the main street, enough money and pride to stimulate the villagers to have a village hall built – complete with a clock tower and weathervane – enough concern over health to persuade them to schemes of water and drainage improvements, sufficient comings and goings along the main road to create no less than three commercial hotels for travellers and drinkers.

The village was then more or less self–sufficient, because travel to town was still relatively awkward and expensive. In 1894 the population, as through most of the nineteenth century, was about 300 persons.

The Baron of Buchlyvie (Christine Thomson)

Today the village can boast a slightly greater population – but not by much. The last census in 1991 shows that 460 people live in Buchlyvie, housed in 195 homes.

Buchlyvie is clearly still a working village, not a retirement village: 26% of Buchlyvie's people are over 60, compared to 20% for the whole of the former Central Region, not a significant difference when the quality of the environment and housing is taken into account. The number of pensioners in the village (33%) is not dramatically greater than in the former Region as a whole (25%)

The under fifteen–year–olds number 18% of Buchlyvie's population compared to 19% for the whole Region. Those in the village who are registered as unemployed account for 3% of villagers versus 7% for the Region.

Buchlyvie has not yet succumbed to the holiday–home syndrome, so widely prevalent where Scottish (or Welsh) villages are situated in beautiful places. Of the 24 "In–Migrants" identified by the census (itself only 5% of Buchlyvie's population) all but eight were identified as coming from elsewhere in Stirling District, and only one from outside Scotland.

The widespread ownership of cars (76% of all Buchlyvie households in 1991) dramatically reduces the village's need for the self–sufficiency of a hundred years ago. The village can still boast a wide variety of skills, professions and craftsmen: the village has two grocers, one of which doubles officially as the village Post Office; it has a butcher and a hairdresser, two flourishing public houses, a number of bed–and–breakfast houses, a garage, a plumber–electrician, a joiner, painters–

and–decorators, a garden centre, a flourishing pottery, and a maker of creative concrete products. While employment on the land is severely reduced in comparison with even fifty years ago, many are still tied to agricultural work.

And there are now new services which have developed since 1900, as a result of the changes to society: doctors, nurses and health visitors operate locally to manage the health of the community and teachers educate the young at the village primary school (compulsory education came as late as 1872). The Mobile Library visits the village, as does the local authority Playbus to entertain pre–school children. Meals–on–wheels operate in the village, and the Post Office provides pension payment and other state benefits.

Other than a little widening here, and a marginal change of direction there, and the building of new houses behind Main Street on both sides of the road, the overall look of the village has modified, but not dramatically changed over the century, as far as the casual visitor is concerned.

Main Street looking west (Christine Thomson)

The Village Name

Research into the origins of the name Buchlyvie have been very inconclusive. It may stem from the Gaelic "Buaidh Chlaidheamh ", meaning 'the victory of the sword', in which case the village commemorates a battle in the dim past. It is possible. Proof is unlikely ever to emerge.

Pronunciation

Historically the village has been spelt in many ways: Bucklyvie, Bollchlyvie, Buchlyvie and even Ballchlavie (by Sir Charles Erskine who was empowered to provide James Graeme, the owner of Buchlyvie lands, with a coat of arms in 1673.) For those not born in the country, the name Buchlyvie is not immediately easy to pronounce. The 'ch' should be pronounced the way Scots pronounce it in the word Loch – and Germans pronounce it in their expression 'Ach !'. The emphasis should be placed on the second syllable, with the first syllable no more than a quiet 'b' sound. The whole word may then sound like "bch–LIE–vi."

Main Street, Buchlyvie: Looking West — Christine J Thomson '96

II
BUCHLYVIE: PRE–HISTORY

In the first 4 billion years of its existence, anyone looking at planet Earth from a spacecraft would have looked in vain to find Scotland. The surface of this planet is a thin skin which floats on molten rock, and the land that came to be called Scotland had a lot of moving to do:

> During Devonian Times (about 400 Million years ago) Scotland occupied a position south of the equator, having drifted northwards from the southern polar latitudes it had occupied before then.The landmass continued to drift northwards through regions corres–ponding to the present day Sahara and into the temperate belt. (BGS Edin))

The evidence for this extraordinary fact lies under the village. Buchlyvie, geologically, sits on a four–mile deep deposit of old red sandstone, which could only have been formed when Scotland was dramatically hotter than today: because it lay near the equator.

From extreme heat, Scotland was then fated to undergo frequent periods of glaciation. In the last of the Ice–ages, about 11,000 years ago,

> ice accumulated on Rannoch Moor and in the high corries of the southwest highlands, and advanced into the lowland areas to reach Callander, Lake of Menteith and Drymen. (BGS)

Then, about 10,000 years ago there was a major warming of the climate, and the ice melted. As the glaciers retreated, a huge lump of ice was isolated, creating the Lake of Menteith (an effect called a 'kettlehole'). The clay, silt and sand that was revealed when the ice disappeared was perfect for the forming of deep layers of peat. But not yet, for,

with the melting of all that ice, sea–levels rose, and the sea came up the Forth basin and flooded the Carse of Stirling (see map). It is even possible that Loch Lomond became a sea–loch in that time.

Eight thousand years ago, tribesmen wandering through the site where Buchlyvie currently stands would have looked across a flat expanse of sea estuary to the Breadalbane Mountains in the North. The rich lands of the Carse of Stirling were only to emerge when, with the fall in the level of the North Sea, the sea water returned eastward.

When the first tribespeople came to the valley of the Forth is not known, but stone–age peoples were in Britain nearly 6,000 years ago. Some would certainly have reached the fertile and relatively accessible Forth basin.

The earliest people here would have been hunters and gatherers; farming came later. The valley slopes to either side of the Forth and Teith rivers would have been too attractive for any early farmers to have ignored.

Sea boundaries c. 11,000 BC (Frank Ellen, after Browne et al.)

The first agriculturalists appeared about BC3000. The first metalworkers – the Beaker People of the Bronze Age – about BC1700. (Martin).

Eventually the Celtic peoples of this part of the world built small settlements and defensive forts – brochs – of which well over 500 have been discovered in Scotland.

The little archaeology undertaken at Buchlyvie – at the Fairy Knowe, half a mile east of the village on the Stirling road – established the existence of an Iron–Age circular house with timber supports for a thatch roof. Carbon dating placed the hut around 100AD. A drystone tower–fort was also unearthed. Additionally, Roman coins were found (Main).

By Roman times, Celtic iron–age peoples called the Dannoni were to be found on the other side of the Campsies in the Clyde valley, and Picts occupied large parts of the Highlands. By the time the Romans departed in c. 400AD, the Picts were moving down to the lowlands; the Angles expanded northward from Northumbria into the Lothians; Britons created the kingdom of Strathclyde with its capital at Dumbarton, which stretched from Argyll down to Lancashire ; the Scots of Dalriada who had come from Ireland then moved into the upper Forth basin, bringing the new Christian religion and setting up monasteries at Aberfoyle and Dunblane; Norwegians invaded the Western Isles and held some of the western seaboard. Such activity must have resulted in frequent clashes and skirmishes for land, power and dominance.

Whatever early settlers there were in Buchlyvie, they could hardly escape the endless traffic of tribes on the move: living as they did on the main route which went from the Irish Sea to the North Sea in the east, the villagers were likely to see travellers and migrants on a regular basis, and not all of them would be peaceable.

With four or five major ethnic groups jostling for land, speaking separate languages and with very different cultural traditions, but with none sufficiently warlike to ensure dominance overall, the relationships between Britons, Angles, Picts and Scots must have ebbed and flowed according to the strength of their chieftains. Not until the Norwegian invaders of the Western Isles threatened all of them, coinciding with the emergence of a strong king among the Scots – Kenneth McAlpine – did these disparate groups, after some major battles, accept union into one nation under one ruler. Overcoming the Picts, McAlpine united the country north of the Clyde–Forth into the single kindom of Alba. "By 1034 all of these disparate tribes owed allegiance to one Alban King" (Smout)

For nearly 200 years the land was ruled by strong kings. David, who had learned kingship in the Norman court of England, and his immediate successors – Malcolm IV, William the Lion, Alexander II and Alexander III – brought to the country the government it needed to give the nation a surer and more peaceful existence: the church was reformed, feudalism introduced, burghs created and government administration properly controlled.

The total population of the country was still very small by today's standards – a few hundred thousand. Buchlyvie was still a very small cluster of cottages, largely peopled by peasantry working on the lands of the lairds, making everything they needed, and their poverty ensured their needs were at survival levels.

Over the ensuing centuries little changed. Population, wages and social customs were virtually stationary. The villagers of Buchlyvie were dominated then, as they were to be until the twentieth century, by the will of the laird, and of the church which supported him. The potential wealth which lay in the land was to remain unlocked until the advent of agricultural reform in the late eighteenth century. Scotland's wealth in its minerals – spectacularly, coal and iron ore – was to have to wait almost as long to be dis–covered. In the meantime the order of the day was survival, in a primitive economy, living a precarious and primitive life.

III
THE BEGINNINGS OF THE VILLAGE 1500-1800

The Community

There are very few references to Buchlyvie as it existed in 1500. Even in the best–recorded societies, a cluster of cottages housing a handful of families, living in a relatively obscure part of a mountainous country is unlikely to feature in historical documents.

Where details may be found are, of course, in those documents concerned with land ownership, the single most valuable commodity in the world until the age of the Industrial Revolution. And so it is in the Scottish Exchequer Rolls that a record exists concerning ownership of "Bochlyfi" lands. It is recorded that the Third Laird of Fintry, one David Grahame had

> ...a sasine of Fintry Striveling in 1495 and Bochlyfi Grahame and Fintre in 1500...(Vol X p771: Vol XI p 465)

In Scots Law a sasine was "the act of giving possession of feudal property" (O.E.D)).

This ownership was to be re–confirmed later, by which time William Grahame –

"the Fourth of Fintry" – had succeded his father in the estates his family held in Stirlingshire and Forfar. Two charters during the reign of James V confirm the ownership of these lands in 1541. The charter grants the 'lands of Bochlyfi Grahame in the Lordship of Menteith and county of Perth... which the King, also for good service and for money paid, erected into the Barony of Bochlyvie Grahame...' (yet another spelling!)

The Grahames of Fintry, living then in their castle, The Mains of Fintry, were to continue in possession of the Buchlyvie lands, even after the misfortune which befell the sixth Laird. Supporting the old religion, he was implicated in a treasonable plot to return Scotland to Catholicism, and was executed in Edinburgh on January 16, 1593.

Fortunately his son David – "Seventh of Fintry" – was too young to be implicated in the affair which killed his father.

He, however, had other troubles:

> He was a devoted loyalist (to the cause of Charles I, then fighting the Round–heads for his survival) and a supporter of his great kinsman, the Marquis of Montrose.... He sold his (Stirlingshire) land to James Graeme, the second Marquis... probably occasioned by the debt which had fallen on the estate through... loyalty to the royal cause..... They (the Grahames) had not only gone beyond their means in assisting the royal army, but had also been fined.... (L.G.Graeme, 1903)

for their carelessness in being on the losing side.

Seal of Rob Grahame of Fintry c. 1430

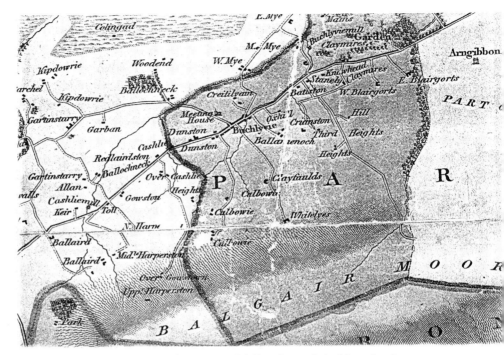

John Grassom Map of Stirlingshire, 1817: Stirling Council Archives Services

Thus the Grahames of Fintry were gone from Buchlyvie by about 1650, after over two hundred recorded years in Stirlingshire, to be replaced by the Graemes of Buchlyvie. Rather touchingly, their affection and identification with this part of the world was such that they continued to refer to their remaining estates in Forfar as "Fintry", and their castle there as "The Mains of Fintry".

At what point Buchlyvie moved from being a small scattering of cottages to being a definable village is not completely clear, but on April 30th, 1672, by a Charter under The Great Seal, Charles II erected the 'town' of Buchlyvie into a Free Burgh of Barony, to be called Buchlyvie–Grahame. George A. Dixon, the Council Archivist, believes that the shape of the village clearly indicates a Carolingian planned settlement. He points to the wide street which allows of street–markets and the regularity of the original cottages fronting the Main Street as typical of pre-Georgian planned villages. The village of Buchlyvie had arrived.

At the same time the village was formally granted a weekly market and two annual fairs – on the 15th June and the 7th of November – for buying and selling horses, cattle, sheep, fish, meal and so on, and its inhabitants were given the right to elect Bailies and any necessary burgh officials. At least as late as 1876, and probably later, Buchlyvie people were still electing a Provost.

> The Town Council and Magistrates of Buchlyvie met on Tuesday evening last in the Red Lion Hotel for the purpose of electing our Provost. Mr John Graham was proposed as a fit and proper person to uphold the honour and dignity of Chief Magistrate of the Ancient Barony of Buchlyvie... (Stirling Journal, 11 August 1876)

Long association of families with places is not at all abnormal. It is difficult for 20th century people to appreciate how little mobility there was before this century provided us with the transport and the attitude that made moving jobs, house and country an easier matter.

No doubt the villagers and farmers of Buchlyvie had histories of association as least as long as that of the Grahames. They simply went unrecorded. Buchanan's guide to the area, first published in 1902 records another such local family:

For 600 years the M'cLachlans resided at Auchintroig (now inhabited by the Kiltegan Fathers). The last of this family, Willam A., died in October 1884.

It was this family, and Auchintroig, that was to feature in one of the Rob Roy incidents connected with Buchlyvie.

While very little is known specifically about Buchlyvie over the three hundred years to 1800, the general conditions which applied to the rest of rural Scotland would have applied here. To quote from Smout:

> ...most people get their living from the land, they are poor, generally undernourished and badly housed, and own little in the way of material possessions; the rate of innovation is so slow that decades and even centuries may go by without appreciable progress...

Because of the climate and the relative poverty of the soil, conditions would have been much harder here than in England.

Sir John Sinclair, writing in 1826 of the Scotland that existed in 1745, could say

> The state of the country was rude beyond conception. The most fertile of tracts were waste, or indifferently cultivated, and the bulk of the inhabitants were uncivilised...The common people clothed in the coarsest garb and starving on the meanest fare, lived in despicable huts with their cattle.

Great expectations for improvement must have been created when the tariff barriers finally came down on the border with England, and the two countries became a common market in 1707. Such expectations were not fullfilled for nearly a hundred years. Relative to agriculture south of the border, the poverty of the soil and the very slow progress of reform in farming meant that the produce of Scottish farms simply could not compete with that of England in quality and price. It was not until the 1760s and the advent of the farming reformers, together with the advent of industrial change, that serious progress was made.

To the general poverty and hard conditions of life for the average citizen of Buchlyvie were added the terrors of plague and famine. One or both might well occur in the lifetime of every villager in Scotland. When they struck, the effects could be terrible. The famine of 1699, after three failed harvests in five years, was estimated to carry off over 20% of the total Scottish population.

Agricultural Reform and Industrial Growth

At the end of this period, however, all the signs for better times started to emerge. Major landlords started to see the possibilities of increased productivity on the land. In the Carse of Stirling, drainage schemes and the removal of 'moss' were soon to transform the upper Forth basin into quality arable land:

> There is no better illustration in Britain of the impact that the pursuit of agricultural productivity can have on the landscape than the Carse of Stirling... The large–scale removal of between three and twelve feet of peat to expose the fertile clay deposits beneath... (led to) a productivity of hay that was up to double that for most other parts of Scotland... (Mathews 1974)

Medieval plough (Frank Ellen, after Elliot)

18ᵗʰ Century Oxen Plough

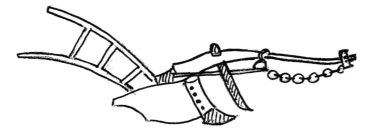

Iron - Chain Plough - Carron Works
circa 1767

Small's Chain plough (Frank Ellen after Elliot)

The North Church, Station Road

As a result, the Carse was to gain a reputation as the hay–basket of Scotland. Once the momentum for change started, Scots proved to be ingenious as inventors and innovators to sustain the improvement.

The old Scots plough was stunningly unwieldy and unproductive: it was about 14 feet in length and took ten oxen and twelve people to operate it. Just half an acre could be ploughed in a day. In 1767 the Scot James Small invented the chain plough which could achieve far greater efficiency and needed only two horses to draw it;

Smith of Deanston invented a more efficient harrow; Stirling and Meikle invented successful threshing machines. Mechanisation had arrived. (Elliott) The big Scottish landlords borrowed freely from the practices south of the border. Enclosure, crop rotation and new crops – clover, potatoes and rye–grass – were among the innovations.

Hand in hand with this agricultural reform was the development of rural textile industries. New inventions here necessitated the use of water as the driving mechanism with which to power the new machines. The textile mills – for cotton and linen – sprang up everywhere where there was fast water. Locally this happened at Balfron, Fintry and Cambusbarron.

The Statistical Account (Vol 9) of the 1790s identifies that Buchlyvie was also involved in the textile boom:

> In Buchlyvie, some of the newly invented jennies for spinning cotton have been set up by a Balfron Company. And in both villages as well as through the parish, a considerable number of weavers have been employed by several companies in

weaving muslins. Such institutions not only give bread at present to many individuals and families, but must in time excite a general spirit of industry and enterpriz (sic).

Maps also show a walkmill for the fulling of wool in Buchlyvie, along the Mye Road leading out of the east side of the village ("Waulkmill" as it is called on the earliest map).

There was, further, a "Tan–work, with sixteen or twenty pools".

All these enterprises, of course, competed for the labour needed to work on the land, and were no doubt responsible for the improvement of conditions and wages locally to recruit and keep such labour in the increasingly competitive job market.

With all the new wealth created, and the general opening up of more land and more factories, more people were needed, not less. One solution was the development of planned villages created by landlords to entice greater numbers to their operations. Fintry, Gartmore and Balfron were largely built under this stimulus.

Session, Managers and Officials,Buchlyvie United Free Church
The Photo is dated Oct 1902, but has no indication of who is being photographed. However, the opposing title page identifies 22 men and one woman under the headings of "Session", "Managers" and other specified officials.(The photo has 22 men and two women, so we assume that the listed people appeared on the photo).

Session

Rev. Wm.S.Cowie, Moderator

Mr James M'Phie, ordained 1860
Mr Alex Morrison, ordained 1873
Mr John More, ordained 1878
Mr George Morrison, ordained 1892
Mr William Bauchop, inducted 1902

Mr John Harvie, ordained 1892
Mr James Dick, ordained 1895
Mr James Risk, ordained 1895
Mr D M'Kerracher, inducted 1892

Managers

Mr Robert More, Preses
Mr John Bauchop Mr David Muirhead
Mr John Campbell Mr Alexander Stewart
Mr John Drysdale Mr James Stewart
Mr James B. Gibb Mr James Taylor
Mr Thos M'Ewen, Treas. Mr John Milne, Clerk

Leader of Psalmody *Mr George Dalgleish*
Harmoniumist *Miss Kate Buchanan*
Church Officer *Mr Daniel M'Lellan*

The Church

For most of the period 1500 to 1800, Buchlyvie had no church. Villagers had, it is assumed, either to walk, or ride, or take their carts to the church at Kippen, in whose Parish Buchlyvie then lay. Then, in the eighty years that followed 1750, Buchlyvie was able to boast of not one, but three churches.

Religious belief was then a matter of the gravest importance to many, if not most, of the Buchlyvie villagers, as it was all over Britain. "The Scottish Reformation was from the first a movement from below, not, as in England, a state–controlled affair". The same source (Parker) identifies Scotland's Catholic church as more corrupt morally and financially than elsewehere in Europe "with many of its clerics incontinent...and a good proportion of its higher offices used for the maintenance of royal and noble bastards." John Knox fought to establish a Calvinist alternative, which became accepted as the new established religion of the country by 1567. While Bishops continued to be tolerated, they, and the Royal (Stuart) power that lay behind the Kirk, continued – in the eyes of many ordinary parishoners across Scotland – to backslide towards the practices which had been the initial cause of the reformation: corruption, forms of worship tending to Catholicism and the hated matter of patronage – where lairds and nobility appointed ministers against the wishes of the local congregations.

When Ebenezer Erskine was ejected from the Established Church in 1740 because he spoke strenuously against these vices, he was to find many supporters in Buchlyvie.

South Church (Frank Ellen)

Erskine sometimes preached at a quiet spot near Honeyholm on the banks of the Endrick, and before long a church was built at Edenbelly not far off....Its first minister was the Reverend John Clelland...Ten years later the seceders from Buchlyvie left that congregation and took the minister with them to become the first minister of the Associate Congregation of Buchlyvie.

Land was bought from the Laird and the North Church, in Station Road, was built to house the congregation.

The work of building proceded in great harmony and self–denial. They gave contributions willingly, in the form of manual labour, and farmers gratuitously undertook the transport of materials. The slates were brought from Aberfoyle on the horses' backs along a track, there being no road. The Church was opened for worship on the first Sunday in May 1752. The total expense was £ 153 and 5 shillings (document celebrating the bi–centenary of the North Church):

Paid to the Laird for ground	£ 5	0	0
Building	£26	3	0
Wood and Wright work	£48	5	0
Slating and Slates	£20	4	0
Lime	£11	0	0
Raising Stones and Sand	£10	4	0
Sundries	£32	9	0
Total	£153	5s	0d

Not everyone in Buchlyvie was a Secessionist, and many must have continued to walk every Sunday to the established Churches of Scotland in Kippen or Balfron. To make worship easier for this group, the Church decided to erect a Chapel of Ease at the east end of the Village (but often referred to as the South Church) and completed the work in 1835. It was made a full parish (quoad sacra) church in 1876.

By that time, however, a further and equally serious break had occurred in the Church of Scotland. In 1843, Thomas Chalmers seceded and walked out with nearly 40% of the Church's ministers, to create a Free Church of Scotland. Buchlyvie's third church was to be a church

for this Secessionary group, which formed a congregation in the 1840s. The *Stirling Observer* of Saturday December 16 1876 reported that

A new Free Church had been built at Buchlyvie, Presbytery of Dunblane. Its material is of iron, and it has every convenience for the comfort both of people and minister...On the Sabbath last the new church was opened by the Rev. Dr Beith.....After a sumptuous tea, partaken of by multitudinous guests with much joyfulness...
the congregation was introduced to the new minister, The Rev Mr Rose.

Built of corrugated iron, this church – standing where the butcher's shop stands today, on the South side of Main Street, facing the junction with Station Road – was pulled down and rebuilt in Dumbarton, when the United Free and the United Presbyterian churches decided to merge in 1899 - a year ahead of The National Union.

The final reduction to one church happened in 1931, when the Reverend Cowie retired as Minister of the North Church and the decision was taken for the two remaining congregations to merge.

Arms Of Clan Gregor (Frank Ellen)

Rob Roy McGregor

Buchlyvie lies only a very few miles south of the Highland mountains. From the point of view of a Highlander bent on cattle rustling (reiver was the term then current), the distance down to Buchlyvie was comfortably within the capabilities of a raiding party.

There was also a tradition, not often proven, that the raiders were not above lifting a woman at the same time, particularly if she was attached to someone rich enough to pay the ransom to get her back, or if she was coveted as a potential wife.

Even when Buchlyvie's livestock was not the target, the raiding party would need to drive the cattle stolen from elsewhere back to their Highland lair along an available road – one of which happened to go through Buchlyvie. The village must have lived in some anxiety over this traffic of bandits.

Among the reivers, the best known were the MacGregors, who had been fighting and raiding since 1300 over the considerable Highland territory they dominated. By 1700 they had lost most of their lands, largely to the Campbells, but the current MacGregor – Rob Roy – was still widely famous for his wildness and general unruliness.

Cattle raids must have happened frequently, and one of them was recorded in the early autumn of 1691.

It is said that information reached Rob Roy that the Earl of Callander and Linlithgow's drovers were to send two

Rob Roy MacGregor (Frank Ellen)

Auchentroig today
(Frank Ellen)

hundred cattle to the Stirling Tryst (market). "Rob Roy's intention was to separate the cattle from the drovers as the herd passed through Buchlyvie." (G.J.Summers)

In the early morning, MacGregor posted his men all over the village to await the arrival of the herd, to the considerable alarm of the inhabitants, who were never very comfortable when even one of these heavily armed highlanders was in the vicinity.

Old Auchentroig
(Frank Ellen)

Highlander Weapons (Frank Ellen)

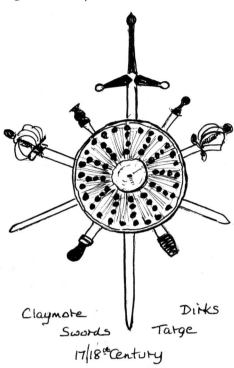

Claymore Swords   Dirks   Targe

17/18ᵗʰ Century

As the day wore on, and still the MacGregors didn't move out of the village, anxious messages were sent out to the men of Kippen and Balfron to provide Buchlyvie with the means to eject the raiders. Now the MacGregors in their turn were becoming concerned about the number of villagers they could see armed with sickles, scythes and pitchforks, collecting nervously in the village. Rob – no doubt wanting to save his men and their energies for the more important rustling to come – withdrew them to the moors above Kippen, where they could still watch the road for the coming of the herd.

When the cattle were spotted at last, the MacGregors descended from the moors, only to discover a body of determined villagers blocking their road. The story has it that Rob Roy ordered his men to attack using only the flat of their swords. The violence of the clash inevitably led to bloodier action. The villagers fell back "before the sharp edge of deftly handled steel", the drovers were killed and the cattle taken.

There is a tailpiece to this story. Rob Roy, annoyed by the interference of the Kippen villagers in what he felt was none of their business, went back to have it out with them. He found the village deserted. So he rounded up their cattle and drove them back to the Trossachs to add to the Callendar herd.

No doubt the consumption of beer and whisky in Buchlyvie was to rise in the weeks that followed, as villagers gathered to talk about the great incident, and regale themselves with the deeds of courage done on the day. The reaction of the Earl who had lost the cattle is not recorded.

Auchentroig

The MacLachlans of Auchentroig inhabited the Auchentroig lands – to the north–west of the village on the way to Aberfoyle – for six hundred years from 1300. In that time probably many houses were built, for the 'Old House' that still stands today only carries the relatively new

Advertising brochure of Auchentroig Homespuns

21

Auchentroig House as a hospital in the 2nd World War

date of 1702, long after the MacLachlans had first arrived. This house was to be the scene for another Rob Roy 'event'.

Having lifted MacLachlan's sheep and cattle, Rob Roy MacGregor besieged this house in a determined attempt to winkle out the Laird. Finding the strong oak door too resistant to his men's blows, Rob Roy resorted to the torch, burning the door badly before smoking the Laird out. MachLachlan had no option but to pay the ransom to get himself freed.

The new house built in 1843 later came into the hands of the Crawford family. They were responsible for extensive reconstruction in 1901. A major fire all but gutted the house in 1923. Those who were village schoolchildren at the time still remember being taken down to watch the house as it burned. A new house was then built which was completed in 1930. The

Crawford family continued to live and work there until the 1960s when the estate was split up and sold off. During the Second World War, the house served as a hospital for allied wounded, mostly Polish. Before selling the house off, the Crawfords had set up and run an enterprise weaving all types of tweed and woollen textiles under the Auchentroig Homespuns label.

The House was bought by St.Patrick's Missionaries (Kiltegan Fathers) in 1965, when they started a school for late vocations.

The Fathers hold an open day annually.

Garden

The other 'Big House' within the vicinity of Buchlyvie is Garden (the emphasis is on the second syllable: Gar–DENN). Like Auchentroig, there is an old and a new house on the estate. In the case of Garden, the old house is now ruined, plundered of its stone to build the newer house. The old house consisted of a moated tower with a drawbridge entry. Sir Duncan Forrester of Garden was Comptroller of the King's Household under James IV (1488–1513) and appears to have been the first Laird of Garden.

The Forresters had sold the estate to Sir Archibald Stirling of Keir by the end of the sixteenth century. As with Auchentroig, Garden was also to have an unwelcome visit from Rob Roy.

He, the story goes, having been expelled from his lands, chose to become a 'contractor' for the policing of the local lands – which appeared to involve what, to modern eyes, seems very like a protection racket. Mr Stirling of Garden had gone off on a visit, together with his wife. On their return they discovered their fortress in the possession of Rob Roy, and the drawbridge up. MacGregor appeared at a window and told Stirling he awaited his 'Black Mail' which Stirling had so far failed to pay. When Stirling adamantly refused, Rob Roy fetched one of the Stirling children from the nursery and held it out of the upstairs window. "The father "says the tale "partly by the entreaties of the mother, was induced to comply with Roy's demands."

The 'New' house, built in 1749, was enlarged in 1828 and since that date the house has remained virtually unchanged. The parklands were planted between 1800 and 1850. The Stirlings acquired the village of Arnprior in the eighteenth century and were the principle Heritors of Kippen Parish Church, of which Buchlyvie was a branch.

Garden house (Frank Ellen)

Estate Plan of Buchlyvie Village in 1850

IV
THE VILLAGE 1800–1900

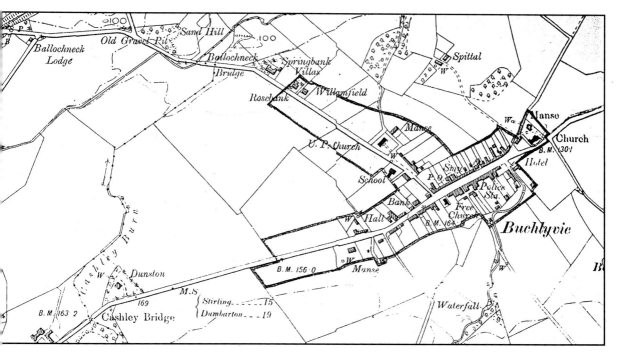

The Community

In 1801, the total population of the Kippen parish (in which Buchlyvie is incorporated) stood at 1,722 persons. One hundred years later that total figure stood marginally changed at 1,456, some 15% less than the 1801 figure.

Buchlyvie's total population was estimated as 313 in 1894 and can be expected to have been little different in 1800. This was not at all the Scottish pattern overall: for the former Central Region of Scotland as a whole, the population for 1901 was 4.5 times greater than the population in 1801: 278,000 in 1901 versus 64,000 in 1801.

With the exception of the size of population, the hundred years from 1800 saw remarkable changes take place in Buchlyvie. They do not seem at all dramatic to us in the twentieth century, but they must

have been so to the villagers of the time.

In 1800 the villagers drew all their water from wells and not even a standpipe was available. Candlepower, peat and wood were the prime village energy sources. Many villagers had a cow or two: often the animals would share the same house, if not the same living space as the people. Sanitary 'conveniences' were nearly all outdoors, and they emptied into cesspits or – often – uncovered drains which ran off into the burns and ditches.

Smallpox, occasional cholera, dysentery, influenza and a hundred other infections went uncontrolled, and killed young children and their parents with random cruelty. Alexander Weir, writing in 1953 about Buchlyvie as it was in 1900, describes an open ditch finally being covered over which had run right beside the Village School, and was

Plan of Buchlyvie Village in 1896

View of Buchlyvie from the East

....blamed for many of the epidemics which periodically visited the village. And again: "at the east end of the village, when the water (in the burn) was low, pollution was rife".

Medical help, like education, was available but only if it could be afforded. The great bulk of the villagers did without either. It is not terribly suprising that the life expectancy of Scots in the middle of the century was only 41 years for males and a year or two more for females.

The Reverend W. Anderson, in his account of the Buchlyvie of 1841 noted that

Main Street looking East, early 1900s

there are two schools, the teachers of which are paid entirely from the schools fees...Reading English is 10 shillings a year ..writing 16 shillings, arithmetic £1 and Book–keeping £1 a year.

The vast majority of Scots were paid under £30 a year (1867), and would find these fees a very heavy burden indeed.

Compulsory schooling came to Buchlyvie – as elsewhere in Scotland – in 1872, though the school took some years more to build. It was only completed in 1876. Medical help on today's widescale basis would have to wait a further seventy years. However, programmes of mass vaccination and innoculation had dramatic effects on the community's survival rate. Enforced vaccination against smallpox started in 1855 and no doubt Buchlyvie took part in it, and benefitted from it.

Despite hardships, people have a knack of making the most of the hardest world. The Reverend W. Anderson, writing the Kippen Parish "New Statistical Account "in 1841 said

The people, on the whole, enjoy in a reasonable degree, the comforts of life, and are contented with their situation and circumstances; and are in general intelligent, moral and religious...

Survival in Buchlyvie in 1850 depended on good luck, and the willingness of the village community to help others in serious need, as problems arose.It also depended on the extent to which the community was willing to solve some of its own problems.

Main Street looking East, showing the junction with Station Road(1904)

Buchlyvie Water Company

The creation of the Buchlyvie Water Company was a classic example of community self–help.

In 1869, a meeting of the village determined on a better water supply, and created the organisation, and found the wherewithal to bring it to fruition. (Sewage disposal was still being resisted 35 years later, because of the cost, and was still to come).

A public meeting in 1869 led to a broad agreement among the villagers that a water scheme was desirable. The Buchlyvie Water Company was set up to create

> a more convenient and plentiful supply of water...which would likely cause a more liberal use, and thus more conducive to health.

A 500 gallon tank with its associated pipe–work was built, with the approval of Mr McKellar, the then tenant of Cashley Farm, from whose land the water was to be drawn. On the 20th January 1870 the undertaking was opened and operating.

In July 1870 the company was officially registered, with a share capital of £150.

Consumers were rated on a rental basis and drew the water from standpipes. In 1886 major reconstruction took place to enlarge the tank and construct filters. Gradually the water supplies became more widely available in the village ; in 1878 to the South Church Manse, in 1880 to the Village Hall. Taylor Place was connected in 1884–5, and the pipe was extended to

Springbank. In 1913 a supply was laid to the Station, and to John Allen's Creamery; the start of Local Authority housing in 1927 led to further extensions.

Plentiful water was to transform the village: by 1894

> Buchlyvie, with a population of 313 (in about 80 households), had 16 water–closets, 12 baths, 10 wash–hand basins, 86 inside sinks and 53 privies. (Mitchell).

The first office bearers of the Company make very clear the local, and democratic, nature of the venture: Dr. Marshall; Walter Parlane (Feuar, at the Post Office); David Harvie (Joiner); Robert McLuckie (Farmer); Robert McIntyre (Contractor and Innkeeper); Alexander Stewart (Millwright in the village); James McPhie (Boot and

The old Buchlyvie Hotel on Main Street

Station Road and Cross, Buchlyvie

Station Road in the early 20th century

when the County Council took over water responsibilities in 1932, and the Water Company was dissolved.

The Village Hall

Approaching the village from the west, the traveller first sees a cluster of cottages, and rising solidly above them, a clock tower with a cupola and weathervane. This is the Village Hall.

As the village moved towards the end of the nineteenth century, local and national documents of the time provide a clear impression that life is getting better for everyone. While many things are not yet as they might be, there is a growing confidence, exemplified in Buchlyvie in the creation of the Water Company, brought about by villagers determined to improve the quality of their life – following the helpful example of Kippen, who had created their own water supply just before Buchlyvie did.

More people were making more money in the village, judging by the number of traders and the building of a branch of the Bank of Scotland at the top of the Main Street, opposite the Rob Roy Inn. In 1860, Slater's Directory identifies a bakery, boot and shoe business, a carrier, a number of

Shoemaker with the Co–Op Shop); Walter McFarlane (Grocer); William Burns; Peter McAlpine (Chairman); George McFarlane (Secretary) and Duncan Keir (Treasurer).

When the Company became a full Limited Liability Company, the first Chairman was Robert McLuckie, a local farmer. Then came John Carrick (Blacksmith at 'Rockhill' cottage) and then David Harvie, the village wheelwright, who held office until 1885. Daniel Fisher Sr of Ballemenoch then became Chairman until his death in 1910. Next came John McOnie (Glenside, originally a draper) to 1918, followed by Daniel Fisher Jr until his death in 1926. The last Chairman was the Reverend G.S.W.Cowie (whose daughter, Miss Kate Cowie, was to be the village schoolteacher for so many years) to the time

Main Street and the village Hall (Christine Thomson)

ROB ROY

Main Street; village Hall, Harvie Tower.   Christine J. Thomson 96

grocers, a miller, a saddler, a blacksmith, tailors, vintners, wrights and carriers, hotels with assorted publicans and cellar–men, in addition to the railway staff, domestics working in the big houses (and one or two in the village), and people assisting in the various shops and workplaces.

While wages would not have been reasonable by twentieth century standards, the possibility of starving to death was now relatively remote, even if hunger could still be found in many of the cottages. Children still went to school in their bare feet, still suffered from rickets due to poor nourishment, but life was distinctly rosier for most people.

With all of this general improvement Buchlyvie people could start to think more often in terms of the community's needs, because they could now worry marginally less about their personal survival. The desire for a meeting place was strong. Churches were plentiful, but no place existed for other village meetings: dances, masonic events, club meetings, evening classes, ladies' get–togethers and so on.

Once again the village took the initiative. A public meeting was held on the 1st February, 1883, chaired by the Reverend John MacDonald, Minister at the South Church. The meeting unanimously agreed the need for a new meeting place. A committee of fifteen was appointed to consider the matter. A subsequent meeting agreed that such a hall should be paid for by public subscription.

Little information is available about the subscribers. Certainly the whole village would have participated. What is certain is that one man, James Harvie of Ballochneck must have made a bigger than average contribution, for the tower of the Village Hall was named after him. All told, it was later revealed, the cost of building the Hall – including the cost of the clock and its bell – had amounted to £1234, 12 shillings and 7 pence.

The foundation stone was laid on the 22nd May 1884 (planners and architects seemed to move very quickly in those days), only twelve months after the first decisions were taken. Less than six months later the Hall was built and was formally opened on the 7th November.

At the laying of the foundation – performed by Mr R.C.Graham Bontine from Gartmore – a bottle was placed under the stone containing the names of the Committee and the subscribers, a copy of the *Stirling Observer* of the day, and some coins.

The Village School

The village school, built in 1876 "under the management of the Drymen and Kippen School Boards "(*Stirling Saturday Observer*, 4 November 1876) had to be extended in 1908. "The Education Act of 1872 made school attendance compulsory from five to

The school (Frank Ellen)

thirteen, though with numerous exemptions and provisions for 'half–time' work. In 1883 the leaving age was raised to fourteen...but children over the age of ten were allowed to work as half–timers if they reached Standard III and were allowed to leave altogether if they reached Standard V." (Smout) This system was not abolished until 1936. In 1945 the school leaving age was to be raised to fifteen.

To this apparently idyllic situation, Smout adds the significant rider

> two–fifths of the children of agricultural labourers are uneducated on account of their being too soon withdrawn from continuous attendance....The minute books of country schools constantly testify to the pressures of harvest, weeding and parental poverty in keeping the children away from school...

In the rural tradition of this time, the children of Buchlyvie would get all their education at the village school up to the age of thirteen, not just to the age of eleven as now applies, for there were few secondary schools available except in the cities.

Alexander Weir could report from his own experiences of the Buchlyvie School house in 1900:

> There were then only two rooms, with a porch at the front for the boys, and a similar apartment at the back for the girls...The majority of the boys wore knickerbocker suits, a cap, washable white collars (which were, of course,

separatable from their shirts, for easy daily washing: Editor) stockings and tackety boots, but in the early summer and autumn a big percentage had bare feet, and much playtime was spent by the unshod on the green opposite the school...The girls wore pinafores with black stockings and sparable (sic.) boots.(1953)

Those who could recall back to 1900 remember the annual outing for the Buchlyvie village children. The Band of Hope and the Independent Order of Rechabites persuaded most of the local farmers to give of their time, wagons, horses and generosity in order that the children should have a memorable day. Farmers decorated their wagons, their wives cut sandwiches and cooked delicacies. The wagons were fitted up with seating, the children assembled and loaded into them, and they set off out to the selected destination.

> It was grand to see the long line of decorated carts and horses moving slowly along, and the happiness of the young trippers...

Alexander Weir reported in the *Stirling Observer* of the 12 October 1953, in *Buchlyvie 50 years ago*. The boys and girls were expected to play separately on such an occasion:

> There were sports and football for the boys, with skipping–rope competitions for the girls...

Buchlyvie Station: Railway Staff

The Forth & Clyde Junction Railway

On the 26th May 1856 the dream of the proprietors of the Forth and Clyde Junction Railway came to fruition with the formal opening of their creation. The station at Buchlyvie (see pages 32 & 33) was built as part of a line which ran from Stirling to the bottom end of Loch Lomond at Balloch, where it met up with another rail system which ran to Dumbarton and Glasgow, run by the North British Railway Company.

No less than 146 Scottish railway companies are recorded in the 19th century, and the North British was much the most dominant in this part of the country: they master–minded the development of a further line branching from Buchlyvie to Aberfoyle, designed to carry freight and tourists, and also a line from Glasgow via Lennoxtown up the Blane Valley to join the Forth and Clyde at Dumgoyne.

The Forth and Clyde company had built the railway in the chief hope of making much money from carrying Fife coal in the east to the Clyde in the west. It would – and did – additionally carry a host of other freight and passengers to and from the stations at which their trains stopped: out of Stirling to Kippen, Gargunnock, Port of Menteith, Buchlyvie, Balfron, Gartness, Drymen, Caldarvan, Jamestown, Balloch and Balloch Pier.

The Reverend W. Anderson notes that the coming of the railway caused the disappearance of the horse–and–coach business. With a rapid increase in use of the railways, the fares became affordable to a growing sector of the population. In the beginning, the fare from Kippen to Stirling was 2 shillings and 3 pence. By 1910 it was no more than 2 pence. In 1856 three trains passed each way, stopping at Kippen and Buchlyvie and at farm halts in between. By 1900 a total of 17 trains passed daily along the railway.

While the single line between Balloch and Stirling retained its name as the Forth and Clyde Junction Railway it operated as a quiet branch of the North British until, in 1923, it was formally incorporated into the bigger company, the L.N.E.R.

It is clear from contemporary records that the railway grew to have a considerable

Dr MacGregor's pony being Shod
Left to right:
Johnnie Campbell, John Morrison, Archie Weir

hold over the public's imagination and affection: steam engines and railway crossings mysteriously stir young passions, and especially male ones. John Thomas, an author whose passion for rail was clearly retained throughout his life – many of these paragraphs owe much to his "Forgotten Railways of Scotland", published in 1976 – says that the village stationmaster had a status not very different from that of the minister, the dominie and the village doctor. He also tells of the pride of staff and passengers in seeking to become the proud winners of the best–kept–station award which North British encouraged among its employees. It appears to have been the tradition that, on hearing from the railway staff that 'the inspector' was about to visit to make his adjudication, commuters would bring along their best geraniums and other plants to deck out the station:

city trains departed leaving a platform display that would not have disgraced Kew.

After the adjudication, the travellers would collect their plants on their way home.

Farming

As in all previous centuries in Buchlyvie, farming and its related activities continued to be the biggest single employer and source of wealth–creation in the community during the nineteenth century.

It was during this period that exports of livestock into England developed into a major source of Scottish wealth. By 1805

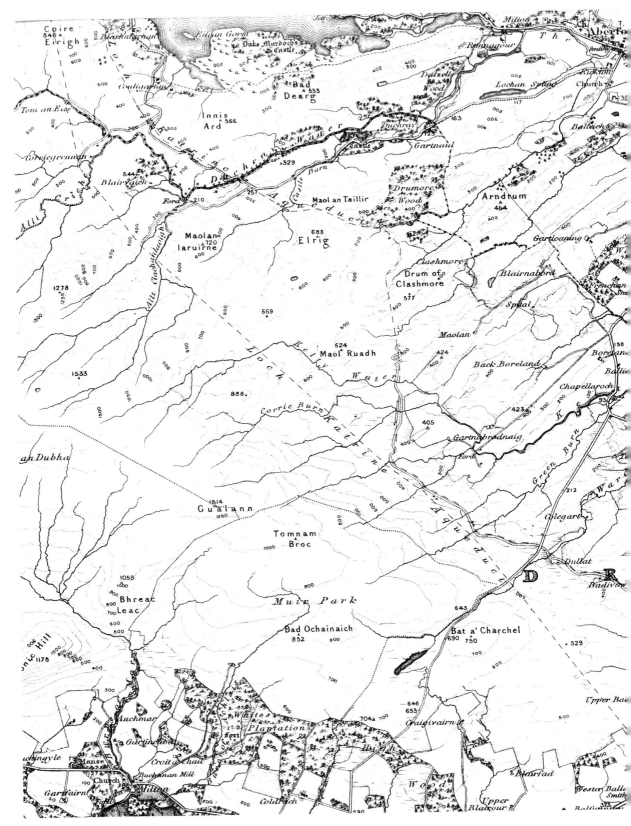

First Ordnance Survey Map 1890 (Reprint series by Caledonian Books of Ellon, Aberdeen)

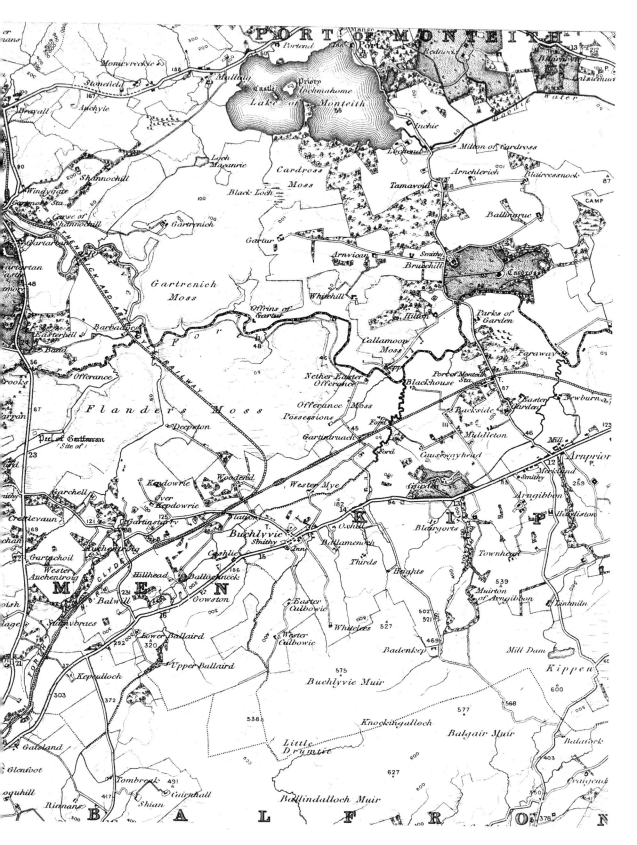

33

Ploughing match at Arngibbon, 1925

Ploughing match at Arngibbon, 1933

Stirlingshire was already nearly 70% enclosed, with the consolidation of the small "runrig" units of farming into larger farms. The Napoleonic wars stimulated the volume of exports to England, as did the rapid growth both in the English and the Scottish population.

Without road transport or railways to carry the cattle south into England, Scottish herds had to be driven by drovers. From all over Scotland, the herds made their way to the major trysts, to be bought by English and Scottish buyers in the exporting trade.

The cattle came down from Crieff to Doune and Balgair, and after Balgair went on to the tryst at Falkirk,

which was then the most famous i: Scotland, handling up to 70,000 head at an one time.

Balgair village – now only a heap o stones – and Balgair Moss, to which th cattle were taken, lie just over the hill from Buchlyvie, towards Fintry. The roads from Kippen, Arnprior and Balfron took th driven cattle to the Balgair Fair. The cattl would spend the night on the Muir, whil their drovers would find lodgings at loca farms:

> Craigend farm charged 2 pence a night, Balafark (a farm–cum–public–house) charged 6 pence, being dearer because it had its own still...The charge was for the drover's meal and drink and, just as important, for his dog's food, too. (Forrester Millar).

Forrester Millar tells us that the last Balgai Fair seems to have taken place in 1890. The rail links to England stopped the need fo these long journeys on the hoof.

Land reclamation and improvement in the Carse of Stirling added very significantly to the importance o agriculture in this area. Sheep now replacec the goat, and the breed of sheep were improved to yield better meat and wool (B.J.Elliott)

With all these beneficial changes, it is no surprising to find growing confidence, as well as wealth, in the farming community in Buchlyvie. One response to this was a

growing self-awareness of their importance, which must have been a major reason behind the creation of an

Ploughing Match at Buchlyvie, 1953

Agricultural Society, a Horticultural Society and an annual Ploughing Match.

Growth in population, and its wealth, together with improved transportation led to other activities: at the turn of the century two new Creameries were built in Buchlyvie. One was Gateside by the railway station and the other on the Mye Road at Shirgarton. There was also the Soor Milk Cairt. It went round the village, making its deliveries. When Oxy (the cart came from Oxhill Farm) ran short of soor milk, he was said to top-up his churns from the burn. A customer complained that she had found a fish in her milk. To this Oxy replied

> Wheesht, or I'll charge you for it as well.

Buchlyvie & Gartmore Agricultural Association

(Notes from David Muirhead, of Wester Arngibbon)

This association was formed as early as 1835 by local farmers with the general objective of having a forum for discussion of agricultural matters of interest to the members. Among other matters, the creation of an Annual Ploughing Match was one of its outcomes. The list of prize winners who were successful in the first such competition, held in 1835, tells us about the farms and the farmers of the time:

1st Prize A.Risk of Cashley
2nd J.Risk of Cashley
3rd prize Wm. MacEwen of Gowston
4th S. More of Culbowie

5th W. Gardner of Kepdowrie

6th John Monach of Garchell

Other farmers who joined in 1835 were Maculloch of Ballaird, McLuckie of Clayfalls, Neilson of Buchlyvie, David Risk the inn keeper, John McEwen the merchant, John Carrick the blacksmith , Alex McAllister the shoemaker, J.McAlpine, J.Risk, J.Parlane, A.McFarlane,David Harvie, Wm.More, Wm.Dalgleish and others.

The first ploughing match was held at Blairgorts, John Zuill's farm.

The first cattle show of the Association took place in 1846, and a variety of prizes was given for stock and for crop cultivation: "Best Two Acres of Purple or Green–top Yellow Turnips ", "Best Acre of potatoes", "Best half–rood of potatoes grown by a Cottar not having a plough" and so on.

In 1847 horses featured for the first time at the annual show, and in later years sheep were also introduced. Later, there were added a Butter and an Industrial sector.

The tradition for a ploughing match had fallen into disuse in the 1860s, coincident with a disastrous cattle plague. The Ploughing Society was founded in 1891 in order to revive the activities of the Agricultural Association.

Some advertisments from
Buchanans Guide to Strathendrick

Two local families of prominence were long connected with the Association, the Fishers of Ballamenoch, with Daniel Fisher being President for many years, and the Stirling family of Garden. In 1924 Sir Steven Bilsland (later Lord Bilsland) became President, holding the post until 1970 when he died. The current chairman is Robert Steel of Wester Mye.

The last cattle show was held in 1938, and was not resumed after the second world war.

Buchlyvie Horticultural Society

This Society was founded in 1885, with prominent patrons from Garden (James Stirling), Gartmore (R.B.Cunninghame Graham), Ballamenoch (Daniel Fisher) and Ballochneck (Gilbert Beith)

The first exhibition was held on the 29th August 1885.

THE LAST HUNDRED YEARS

The Community

Memories in the current Buchlyvie community easily go back to the 1930s; a few to the 20s and the last hundred years have been thoroughly photographed. To that extent the rest of this publication should, and will, consist mostly of reminiscences and photographs.

Thanks to a small number of local writers, the people of Buchlyvie and their customs since 1900 are on record. Prominent among the writers is Alexander Weir, who tells much about the place over these years. A good deal of what follows is to be found in back copies of the *Stirling Observer,* for whom he wrote long articles in the 1950s in which he looks back to the turn of the century.

The Church

At the turn of the century, most of Buchlyvie's villagers attended church regularly and the churches were crowded. Of the Kippen church it was said that

. . . .there are only 4 or 5 free sittings. The seats are divided among the heritors, according to their respective valuations, who, after reserving family seats for themselves, have appropriated the rest for their tenants (Anderson).

No doubt the same was true at Buchlyvie. At the end of the century Scotland is a significantly less devout nation, and there are no seating problems anywhere.

Around the turn of this century, three non–Catholic churches still drew Sunday congregations from Buchlyvie, though two of them – the North church on Station Road (United Presbyterian) and the Tin Church on the Main Street (Free Church) were to amalgamate shortly to become the United Free Church. When the merger happened the congregations agreed to hold services in the North Church. The Tin Church was dismantled, carried to Dumbarton, and rebuilt there.

In 1931, on the retirement of the minister of the United Free Church, the Reverend G. W. S. Cowie, the two remaining Churches agreed to merge. The initial practice of alternating places of worship between the North and so–called South churches had to stop when examination of the North Church revealed it was no longer safe to use. Sadly it has remained unused ever since.

To mark another facet of change since 1900, the current incumbent at the South Church is a woman, the Reverend Moira MacCormick.

North Church, Station Road

South Church (Frank Ellen)

Winners of the Ploughing Match, 1954

blockade of the British coast against imports and the reduction of labour available for the land, added very significantly to the nation's understanding of the importance of home–grown food production.

The tractor started to come in to Buchlyvie as a direct stimulus of the First World War. As a result, the long and splendid history of the horse as the farmers' hardest–working labourer rapidly declined.

The Ploughing Match and the Cattle Show continued to be the big events of the farming community. The cattle show was normally held on the last Saturday in June. For this meeting the village did its best to clean itself up, with much weeding of pavements and whitewashing of most of the cottages. A pipe band was engaged for the day, parading through Main Street before going on to the showfield.

The Horticultural Society also had their big day, usually on the last Saturday in August, and the show was held in the Village Hall. Alex Weir says

> Gardening being almost a necessity, competition was keen and attendances good. One large class which always attracted a large entry was that for the bouquets made up by children.

Farming

The last hundred years has seen no diminution in the importance of farming as a local activity, though progressive improvements in agricultural technology have dramatically reduced the number of people working on the land: from 14% in 1900 to under 10 % in 1951, and to less than 1% of the Scottish population by 1990.

Smout notes that in 1840 it took 22 man–days a year to tend an acre of barley, only 12 days by 1914. By 1958 the figure was down to 3.

Two world wars, with an enemy

The Ploughing Match Committee, (Left to Right: David Bruce (observer), Alec Gunn, D.J. Muirhead, Robert Armstrong, Alan Dykes and Willie Martin Front: John Brisbane, David Young, David Muirhead)

The Baron of Buchlyvie

If the horse was one of the commonplaces in the community in the early twentieth century, then the shire–horse was prominent as the work–horse of farming. Buchlyvie has a particular, and somewhat strange place in the Scottish history of this animal, for it was the birthplace of one of the most famous – and certainly the most expensive – shires ever to be bred. The Baron of Buchlyvie, a magnificent Clydesdale, was bred in Buchlyvie by William MacKeich, farmer at Woodend, in 1903.

No doubt the name given to the horse was drawn from Sir Walter Scott, who mentions it in an 'old Scottish rhyme ' he placed at the head of his 28th chapter of *Rob Roy*:

Baron o' Buchlyvie
May the foul fiend drive ye,
And a' tae pieces rive ye,
For biggin sic a toon,
Whaur ther's neither horse meat
Nor man's meat, nor a chair to sit doon.

(The Baron mentioned in this verse is traditionally believed to be Sir Andrew Graham, second son of the Marquis of Montrose, who is supposed to have founded the village in 1680.)

By the time the Baron was two years old he was already clearly destined for history, for the horse was winning every show in which he was entered. Another famous breeder of Clydesdales, James Kilpatrick, spotted the potential in the young colt and attempted to buy him at the Doune Show. MacKeich turned down the offer. MacKeich later changed his mind, and The Baron went to Kilpatrick after the horse won the Aberdeen show. The price was £ 700.

Another horse–breeder, Dunlop, persuaded Kilpatrick to sell him a half share in the animal. When it became increasingly clear that the animal had great earning capability, Dunlop told Kilpatrick that he would like to buy him out of his half–share. A price of £2000 was agreed between them as the price required for Dunlop's outright ownership. A later court–case indicated that Dunlop believed

The Baron of Buchlyvie

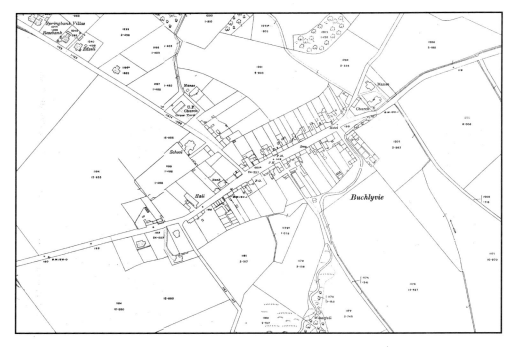

this sum to be Kilpatrick's estimate of the total value of the horse, and that £1000 from Dunlop would secure Kilpatrick's half–share in the animal. Kilpatrick protested that Dunlop must pay £2000 to secure his HALF–share, and that Dunlop had clearly 'misunderstood' the deal. As a result of this disagreement Kilpatrick then called off the whole deal.

In the meanwhile the Baron was earning his living. He earned £60 each time he was put to a mare, and a further £60 should the union prove fruitful. He averaged around two hundred and fifty offspring a year, from an estimated four hundred coverings. As only a part of the year was possible for this activity, the Baron appears to have been vigorous, fruitful and the source of a very significant income to the joint owners.

Unconvinced he was receiving the payments due to him, Dunlop sought redress through the courts. The eventual outcome was an agreement that the Baron should be put up to auction and half the proceeds go to each of the two owners. Dunlop enlisted an anonymous bidder to

Mrs Duncan, a porters wife, and the Station at Buchlyvie, 1950

bid on his behalf, and ended up bidding £9,500, against the then all–time record of £3,000 for the sale of a Clydesdale stallion.

Not very long after the court–case, with all its attendant publicity, the Baron had to be put down in June 1904 after having his leg broken by a mare. His body was subsequently exhumed, and his skeleton went on show as a major attraction in the Glasgow Art Galleries, where it remains to this day in an exhibit which includes memorabilia associated with the animal.

The Closing of the Railway

Alexander Weir, writing in the *Stirling Observer* in 1953, remembered that Buchlyvie Junction was a busy station, with seventeen trains a day on the single line, and a "regular coming and going between the various farms and the station, the railway being the only means of transporting farm produce and bringing the necessities for the feeding of stock and the cultivation of the land."

The trains also carried passengers, including a number of village children to Glasgow schools. The passenger wagons appeared to be deficient in heating, and must have been bitter in the winter months.

The Baron of Buchlyvie (Christine Thomson)

At Dumgoyne station a few warming pans were available for distribution to the freezing children, and it is told that they vied one with another in looking pathetic as they put their heads out at the station, trying to impress station staff that they were especially deserving cases.

And then came the motor–car. The first car in the area belonged to James Reoch, of Gartinstarry. If it passed the village school during one of the break–times, all the children would run to the school railings to peer out at this new wonder as it rattled and roared down Station Road.

Buchlyvie Station

*Gartinstarry
(Frank Ellen)*

Motor buses appeared around the 1920s, when Campbell of Aberfoyle began a regular service on Thursdays to the market. Trucks arrived at much the same time. As the railways had previously killed off the coaching trade, so now road transport would in due course kill off the railway.

John Thomas, railway enthusiast and recorder of the history of Scottish rail, reports on the death of the Forth and Clyde Junction Rail line of the North British:

Throughout its life through–trains from Glasgow to Aberfoyle had served the Blane Valley stations of Lennoxtown, Campsie Glen, Strathblane, Blanefield and Dumgoyne (passing through Buchlyvie to reach Aberfoyle)...In the closing years, the through trains were discontinued. The basic service terminated at Blanefield and a separate train – the Sentinel steam railcar – ran from there to

*Bus in Beech Walk
near Gartinstarry*

Aberfoyle and back...On a sunny Saturday in June 1951, with very cheap fares on offer, this train conveyed only two passengers and a few slim rolls of newspapers..On Saturday the 29th September of that same year, so many passengers turned up at Glasgow Queen Street station that the booking office ran out of tickets. It was the last day of the line.

The Forth and Clyde Junction Railway had been created in the hope of heavy coal transport from Fife, and it never materialised. It had hoped for much local traffic, but the total population it served in the parishes through which it passed totalled only 8,288 people in 1881 (Buchlyvie's population then was 339). After ten years of independent operation the Directors of the venture leased the line to the North British Railway Company. The profitability of the line must also have been reduced by what today would be called over–manning (see the photo on page 30) In 1903, Buchlyvie station staff, according to Alexander Weir, consisted of a Stationmaster (J.B.Gibb), two signalmen, a joiner, a blacksmith and his mate, a

The Village Hall as a hospital in the 1st World War

linesman, a signal fitter, a permanent way inspector and a station porter, excluding "men on the lengths and in the flying squad". A dozen men per station on the books for just a dozen or so trains a day seems, in hindsight, a little excessive.

The Village Hall

Hames Tower Buchlyvre   F. Buchan 2nd Oct 78

The Village Hall

The Village Hall has more than justified the original Committee and subscribers, who had hoped it would serve as a useful focus for the community. It has been used ever since with great frequency and for many purposes.

The Hall serves today as the regular setting for meetings of the Community Council and other local committees, as a play group for the youngest in the village, as a focus for many of the local dances and other celebrations and as a place for special events such as charity bring–and–buy sales.

The building of the Hall led to the creation of the Buchlyvie Operatic and Orchestral Society which functioned for many years in the presentation of plays, concerts, musicals and other stage productions. The annual Christmas Pantomimes which have been held for many years since the Second World War have continued this tradition, though they are now presented by the Scottish Women's Rural Institute.

In the First World War the Hall was put to use as a recovery hospital for men wounded at the front.

In May 1984 the Hall was extensively damaged by fire. The repair included refurbishment and a considerable extension to the original plan.

The War Memorial

It is not known if, or how many, villagers died in the past as a result of the intermittent famines and plagues during the early centuries, or of malnutrition, influenza and cholera in the nineteenth.

The War Memorial on Main Street

The twentieth century, which should have been free of all killing plagues, managed in 1914 – 1918 to find another infection to kill off the population: World War. The monument at the east end of the village is a memorial to the loss of twenty-three men of Buchlyvie in the worst disaster the village has probably ever experienced. This total must be nearly half of those who were eligible and fit to be called up to the front – some fifty or so male villagers.

While, no doubt, Buchlyvie suffered no more than most other British (or French or German) communities of the time, the horror of it can only be appreciated if we understand it in these terms: that nearly half the able bodied young men of the village died during those years:

Robert Alexander, James Bradshaw, Alexander Cowan, George Cumming, William Donaldson, John M. Fleming, Charles Gorrie, John Gray, James Harrison, James Jaffray, John Johnstone, Alfred McFarlane, Alexander McIntyre, Andrew McLaren, William McLellan, Moses More, John Morrison, Ronald J. McOnie, Archibald McVicar, James Scott, Thomas Smith, William F. Steel, George West.

The Second World War was, mercifully, less bloody for Britain. Buchlyvie – with much the same population as in 1914 – suffered just two deaths: David Duff and William Irvine.

School

In 1996 the school teaches 43 children from the area. The Head Teacher is Miss Ritchie and she is supported by Mrs Anderson.

Buchlyvie School Group 1920

BACK, Left to Right: *Miss Armour, M.Parlane, ?, E.Higgins, E.McIntosh, M.Risk, ?, B.Beaton, Mr Abbey*
2nd Row: *? , W. Crombie, ? Ramage, P.McCallum, H.Cameron, A.J.Stewart, D.Donaldson, I McLaren.*
3rd Row: *? , M.Ramage, J. Roy, B.McCallum, A.McCallum, N.Beaton, J.Cameron, J.Higgins, N.Roy, T. McCallum, C.McIntosh*
FRONT: *W.Kirkland, M.McCallum, W.McDowell, M.Wilson, A.Letham, .Duff, D.Duff, R.Stewart.*

Buchlyvie School Group 1935

BACK, left to right: *Miss Cowie, John Carmichael, Geroge Boden, R.Steel, Chris. Wilson, Mary Cameron, Cathie Cameron, Florence Brisbane, George Brisbane, Tom Bennie, Alan Wilson, David Steel, MrLockhart*
2nd ROW: *Jean Hall, Cathie Gallacher, ? Graham, Rena Gorrie, John Cameron, Molly Menzies, Mary Barrett, William Livingstone, Helen Barrett, Nicol Cafferty, Jessie Bennie, Anne Menzies, Betty Coburn, Cathy Smith.*
3rd ROW: *Rita Wilson, Isa Baker, Annie Inglis, Phoebe Gorrie, Helen Cafferty, Roy Stewart, Catriona McCaig, Annie McLachlan, Jean Bennie, Margaret McLachlan, Margaret Buchanan, John McIntyre, Agnes Steel, Sarah Cafferty, Isa Steel, Elsie Bennie, Betty Bennie.*
FRONT: *Aubrey Beaton, William Gill, George Bennie, Daniel Hall, Norman Morrison, J. Morrison, George Steele, Donald McCallum.*

Opposite, upper

Buchlyvie School Group 1925

BACK: *? , J.Duff, M.Parlane, M.Shields, M.McLachlan, K.Morrison,*
2nd Row: *A.Wilson, N.Roy, P.Shearer, E.Higgins, E.McIntosh, I.Duf, M.Wilson, D.McCallum, Mr Tait*
3rd Row: *J.Stewart, T.McCallum, J.Cameron, M.McCallum, A.McCallum, E. McLachlan*
FRONT: *A.J.Stewart, R. Morrison, J.Monach, W.Crombie, A.Livingston, W.Kirkland*

Opposite, lower

Buchlyvie School Group 1926

BACK: *Mr Tait, Peter McCallum, Stewart Mackie, Willie Wilson, Norman Farquhar, D. McCallum, Alec Bennett. Jim Higgins.*
MIDDLE: *Molly Cafferty, Jean Higgins, Nan Kirkland, Cathie MacIntosh, Jean Morrison, Peggy Shearer, Mary Wilson, Mary Shields, Sheena Risk, Cathy Craig, Helen McLachlan, Stewart McLaren*
FRONT: *Jean Dickson, Robert Morrison, Hugh Cameron, Alec Cochrane, John Cafferty, Betty Hutchison.*

Buchlyvie School Group 1956

BACK ROW, left to right: *B.McCrirrick, B.McCallum, M.Mansfield, S.McCallum, W.Elliot, D.Stewart, A.McArthur, P. Mulberay, R.Orr, P.McNee.*
MIDDLE ROW: *I. Gellatly, G. Pattison, H.Bell, R.Irvine, E. McIntyre, I.McCallum, N.Kirk, M. Riley, J.Curtis.*
FRONT ROW: *D.Steel, B.Sneddon, A.Galloway, L.Strang, U.Risk, J.McNee, E.McArthur.*

Buchlyvie School Choir 1966, With Shield won at the Burns Festival, Kippen.

BACK ROW, left to right: *Walter Bilsland, Marie Bennie, William Bennie, Valerie McFarlane, George Bennie Mary Duff, Stewart McNee.*
MIDDLE ROW: *Andrew Buchanan, Susan Oswald, Catriona Murdoch, Alison Murdoch, Hilary Retson, Janet Train, Ann Smith, Anne Johnstone, Anne Laing, Anthony McCallion.*
FRONT: *Jill Hamilton, Ian McKenzie, Joyce Beaton, Janice Brown, William Smith, Kirsty Duff, Gillian Pollock Billy Miller, Isobel Bennie*

Buchlyvie School Group 1996

1	Steven Butler	P.1	14	Graeme Orr	P.1	27	Michael Scobie	P.2
2	David Steel	P.1	15	Ross Jenkins	P.3	28	Emily Scotson	P.4
3	Eilidh Weir	P.6	16	Fraser McKay	P.5	29	Dawn Ritchie	P.7
4	Jennifer Moffat	P.4	17	John Hall	P.6	30	Melanie Grant	P.3
5	Kim McLaren	P.1	18	Stuart Maclellan	P.4	31	Robert McAllister	P.2
6	Jessic Gleave	P.4	19	Eleanor Oswald	P.6	32	Elizabeth McKinnon	P.6
7	Emma McLachlan	P.1	20	Kimberley Buchanan	P.7	33	Louise Ferguson	P.7
8	Christopher Wallace	P7	21	David Miller	P.1	34	Connor Ritchie	P.2
9	Lyndsay Owens	P.4	22	Campbell Buchanan	P.5	35	Jodie Ritchie	P.3
10	Amy Simpson	P.1	23	Andrew Butler	P.3	36	Helen Middlemass	P.6
11	Steven Moffat	P.6	24	Patricia Hall	P.7	37	Jordan Pratt	P.2
12	Pawel Maciejski	P.7	25	Kenzie Gleave	P.6	38	Elaine Jenkins	P.4
13	Paul Ritchie	P.5	26	Lewis Jenkins	P.1			

*Not Present in the photo : Dawn Grant P.1, Jordan Ritchie P.2, ì
Danielle Faller P.2, Kay McLachlan P.3, Greg Cafferty P.5*

J.R.B.

Women's Rural Institute 21st Birthday, 1940.

BACK ROW, Left to Right: *Mrs Roy, Mrs Leonard, Mrs Buchanan, ?, Miss Menzies, Mis Denholm, ?, Mrs McQuiston, ?, Mrs McKinley, Mrs Walker, Miss Smitton, Mrs Cafferty, Mrs Bennie, Mrs Brisbane, Mrs Wilson, ?, ?, Mrs Risk.*
MIDDLE ROW: *Mis McCara, Mrs Dykes, Miss Dykes, ?, Mrs Young, Mrs Boydale, Miss Mcpherson, Mrs Keddie, Miss Morrison, Mrs Sneddon, Miss Mitchell, Mrs Steel.*
FRONT ROW: *Mrs Morrison, Miss Cowie, Mrs J.Morrison, Mrs McFarlane, Miss Howard, Miss I McEwen, Mrs McArthur, Mrs Harvie, Miss Steel, Mrs Beaton.*

Buchlyvie S.W.R.I. Diamond Jubilee, June 12th 1979 in Winnock Hotel, Drymen.

Left to Right: *Mrs Farquharson (Group President), Mrs Murdoch (Federation Vice President), Mrs Oswald (Secretary), Miss Cowie, Miss Harvie and Miss Steel (All founder–members), Mrs Lumsden (Chairman, Central Council), Mrs Morrison (Federation Secretary) and Mrs Duff (Buchlyvie President)*

Scottish Women's Rural Institute.

All the papers concerning the founding of the Buchlyvie Branch of the Scottish Women's Rural Institute were destroyed when the house at Auchentroig was burned down in 1923. R.K.Crawford, writing from Hampshire on the 23rd July 1949, tells the story of its foundation on the 16th July 1919:

> I had been worrying what could keep us together when the 1914–18 war was ended and our work in connection with it i.e the hospital (set up in the Village Hall) and the wonderful number of garments and comforts which Buchlyvie had made for the Red Cross...One morning I received a magazine about the start of Women's Institutes in Canada...I got in touch with those who could provide me with more information. So we in Buchlyvie became, I think, the second S.W.R.I. in Scotland. The first was founded in Fife. The initial meeting was well supported, and we went on from strength to strength...

Mrs Ewan Crawford of Auchentroig was elected the first President in 1919. They chose as their emblem the famous Clydesdale horse The Baron of Buchlyvie.

The Institute meets on the second Tuesday of every month from September

Buchlyivie United Football Club Champion five-a-side team in 1908.

BACK ROW: James Cant, Sam McQueen, Wm Weir, Arch Cant.
FRONT ROW: J. G. Stewart, Andrew Harvie

Buchlyvie F.C: 1933 Cameron Cup Dinner

BACK ROW: Mr McKenzie, J.Duff, P.Tait, P.McCallum, G.Duff, W.Crombie.
MIDDLE ROW: A.J.Stewart, J.Montgomery, J.Camerom, R.Stewart, J.Willis, Ned Harrison, Mr Finlayson.
FRONT ROW: R.Morrison, Mrs Morrison, J.McArthur, A.Carmichael, D.Montgomery, Miss Finlayson.

Opening of Village Playing Field: Football Match 1977, Silver Jubilee Celebrations.

BACK ROW: *Ewan McIntyre, Ian McFarlane, D.Honeyman, E.Stewart, Billy Honeyman, Nicol Cafferty, A.Crombie, J.McGregor, D.McNee, R.Steel*
MIDDLE ROW: *Adam Kirkpatrick, E.Harrison, Peter Robinson, J.Simpson, J.McKeitch, Eddie Mayhew*
FRONT ROW: *J.Crombie, A.McKenzie, Alistair Scott, Billy Gordon, Willy Mayhew, Alan Bates, Fred Chandler*

Colonel Crawford Teeing–Off at the opening of the Village Golf Club, May 1922

to May. Perhaps its key, though not its only activities, are handcrafts and drama productions. The annual pantomime has been the responsibility of the Institute for the last twenty–five years. Its productions have been crowned in the past with top drama awards. Awards in handcraft-shows also regularly come the way of S.W.R.I. village members. Jennie Steel, the current President, still considers that despite these successes,

> the hand of friendship and a warm welcome will always be its main achievements.

Buchlyvie United F.C.

The football team is a considerable focus of attention in the village. Buchlyvie United's beginnings can be traced back to the turn of this century. Alexander Weir, writing in the *Stirling Observer* of November 4th 1954, is once again the invaluable source of information:

> In 1903, James G.Stewart came from the Dollar district to commence business as a plumber....Previously he had played football with King's Park, Stirling, Alloa Athletic, and

THE TEAM....

....PROTECTING THEIR PROMISE OF A WIN.

Buchlyvie Football Club:1995 team (Billy Pretorious)

Opening of the Golf Course, May 1922

Curling Pond at Ballochneck

Village bonfire to celebrate the coronation of King George VI in 1936

St. Johnstone, Perth, and immediately he had settled down (in Buchlyvie) he began to create an enthusiam, and by example set about creating a standard of play which was to prove itself. A club was formed under the name "Buchlyvie United" and it obtained a playing pitch known as "The Bowl" on Cashley Farm...

Excluding periods of enforced hibernation, when the nation was at war, the game continues to be played regularly in the village to the present day, having been re–started in 1947, after the Second World War. Next year (1997) that club celebrates the 50th anniversary since it re–started.

The current football pitch was inaugurated in 1977. Following modern marketing fashions, the team has an official sponsor in the Buchlyvie Inn (formerly the Red Lion) which contributes the team shirts.

Golf

Today the village does not have a golf course, but it did have one some years ago. On the 5th May 1922, a new golf course was opened by Col. Crawford of Auchentroig. The following year a putting green was installed.

Curling and Summer Ice

The Scottish weather lends itself to the sporting use of frozen ponds and lakes. As everywhere in Scotland, the village takes to the ice for curling when the weather is good (or bad) enough to make it possible. A pond at the back of the Spittal, set aside years ago for this activity, refused to freeze even in the sharpest temperatures, so

Consecration of Lodge Buchlyvie No. 1268 of the Freemasons, 17th September 1921

BACK ROW: John Spittal, William McDowall, Dougald Laing, Peter McIntyre, Alexander Cameron, Andrew Shearer, Alexander Weir, Archibald Millett, George Duff, Edward Harrison, Malcolm McCaig, James Brown.
2nd ROW: ?, John Burns, George Dow, ?, William Richardson, Daniel Fisher, ?, ?, ?, Rev G.W.S.Cowie, John Morrison, Hugh Beaton, James Weir.
FRONT ROW: 4th from left: The Provincial Grand Master, Mr Dyer of Alloa.
5th from left: Peter Hay, First Master of the Lodge
(All the rest are unnamed in the photograph)

Halloween Party in the Village Hall c1936

Names of Some Present: Doris Baker, Granny Baker, Isobel Baker, Mrs Baker, Aubrey Beaton, Betty Bennie, Elsie Bennie, Bunty Brisbane, John Brown, Peggy Buchanan, Ellen Cafferty, Helen Cafferty, Annie Cameron, Babs Cameron, Catherine Cameron, David Cant, John Carmichael, Mr Andrew Carmichael, Margery Dun, Phobe Gorrie, Lisbeth Graham, Anne Greenaway, Daniel Hall, Jean Hall, Claire Leonard, Dolly Leonard, Jimmy Leonard, Catriona McCaig, Betty McGill, John McIntyre, Mrs McKinley, Ishbel Porter, James Porter, Mary Porter, Violet Smith, Agnes Steel, Bobby Stewart, Agnes Turpie, Mr J Walker (Headteacher), Margaret Wallace, Chrissy Wilson.

traditionally the village had permission from the owners of Ballochneck to use MacGregor's pond on that estate.

Buchlyvie's Curling Club was officially instituted around 1860 and was admitted to the R.C.C.C in 1865.

A miniature version of curling, Summer Ice, played on a polished table – 22 foot long by 2ft 6inches wide – using metal sliders as substitutes for curling stones was said to originate with the Irish who came to build the new Glasgow–Loch Katrine water supply pipeline, a heroic engineering feat of the mid nineteenth century. The Buchyvie Summer–Ice table is housed in the village hall for the regular league matches against teams from Gartmore,

Donald Fisher, of Ballamenock, on his wedding day

Aberfoyle and Kippen. There are about twenty–five members of the Buchlyvie Summer Ice Club in 1996. Originally the league was considerably bigger, with teams also from Thornhill, Stronachlachar, Brig o' Turk, Killearn and Kinlochard.

Quoits

Around the turn of the century much mention is made of enthusiam among all ages for the game of quoits, in which circular metal quoits were thrown at a post. When metal quoits were not available, horseshoes were considered a reasonable substitute. This pitching sport was sufficiently popular in Buchlyvie to warrant a permanent quoiting ground "with three lines ". Alex Weir claims that it was the advent of football in the village that brought about the game's demise. The quoiting ground was situated close to the current Farmers Shop at the east end of Buchlyvie, on the south side of the road going to Stirling.

Malcom McCaig, of the Rob Roy Hotel, attempted to revive the sport in the 1930s.

Freemasons

Lodge Buchlyvie 1268 on roll of the Grand Lodge of Scotland was founded on the 5th May 1921. Originally the Freemasons met in the Village Hall, but following the fire in the hall in May 1984, they moved to Kippen when the hall was being refurbished. The Lodge has been dormant since the end of November 1993.

Order of the Eastern Star

On the 24th November 1951 a new Chapter of the Order of the Eastern Star was inaugurated – Buchlyvie Chapter 513. It continues to meet regularly in the Village Hall, and has male and female members.

The Children and Old Folk's Committee:

is a historical amalgamation of groups of villagers involved in various benefactions to the village. For example the Children's Committee emerged from the Lighting Committee whose task had been to bring street lights to Buchlyvie at the turn of the century. The Old Folks Committee grew out of the need to manage surplus money from the George VI Coronation Fund. The two Committees are now joined and are called the Children and Old Folks Entertainment Committee

Buchlyvie Brownies

First Buchlyvie Brownies have been active in the village for many years. In 1996 there were eight children in the pack, led by Mrs Margaret Sparkes.

Draughts Club

The village used to have a Draughts Club which ran an annual New Year Ball.

Buchlyvie's Administration

In 1996 the governance of Buchlyvie is in the hands of:

At the EUROPEAN level: The Member for the European Parliament representing Buchlyvie is Mr Alec Faulkner (Labour).

In the HOUSE of COMMONS: The Member of Parliament representing the village is The Right Hon. Michael Forsyth (Conservative), Secretary of State for Scotland.

At the COUNCIL level: The Councillor representing the village on the Stirling Council is David Davidson (Conservative).

At the COMMUNITY level: The Community Council, representing the views of the village to all higher levels, consists of the following members:

Chair: Mrs Jane Fleming
Vice–Chair: Lady Jennifer McLellan
Secretary: Mrs Gena O'Brien
Treasurer: Mr Ken McKenzie
Member: Mr David MacNee
Member: Mrs Jean Buchanan, *Stirling Observer* Village Correspondent.

Main Street c1955

Main Street and the junction with Station Road, before 1963

Village craftsmen c 1950 (Andrew Dun, Eddie Harrison, Wade McColl and Jimmy Montgomery)

Rob Roy Pub, Main Street (Billy Pretorious)

The Village Lollipop–Lady (Billy Pretorious)

BUCHLYVIE PEOPLE

In the process of compiling this book, the names of many village people turned up. While the list is only a small proportion of all those who lived in Buchlyvie over the centuries, it was felt that the villagers would be interested to see them listed, rather than leave them out. It is *not* meant to be a comprehensive list: that would have taken much more research - and, anyway, would probably have filled up all the pages available in this book.

Abbey A.G.	Schoolmaster: 6th Treasurer BWC to 1923
Alexander, John	Boer War veteran, c1900: Had a monkey
Anderson, John	Grocer c 1900
Baker, Mrs (Granny)	Tea room in the 1930s
Ballantyne, William	Retired
Bauchop, William	Farmer 'Lower Kepdowrie' c 1900
Beath, Mr	Chair: Village Hall C/Tee 1884–6
Beaton, Hugh	Butcher: Buchlyvie Freemason
Beck, Alex	Farmer ' Polybaglet' c 1900
Beck, Isaiah	Station Rd. Stonemason c 1900
Berry, The Rev James	Minister at the North Manse c1870
Bishop, James	Saddler in 1860
Bontine, The Hon Mrs	Gartmore c1870
Brown, John	Butcher in the 1930s
Brown Mrs	Confectionery & Tobacconist 1930s
Brown, James	Buchlyvie Freemason
	Baker vanman, roadman, Buch Wat Co
Brown, William	Farmer 'Spittal' c 1900
Buchanan in Woodend	Manager to build North Church
Buchanan of Gartinstarry	Manager to build North Church
Buchanan, Alexander	Grocers/Shopkeepers in 1860
Buchanan, Andrew	'Benard': Director Buch Water Co
Buchanan, Miss Maggie	Ladies Tailor c 1900
Burden, Peter	Brewer/Beer Wagon delivery: Director BWC
Burns, John	Saddler: Buchlyvie Freemason
Burton, F	Jeweller: Taylor Place shop c 1900
Cameron, Alexander	Benard: Ironmonger/Plumber 1930s
	Buchlyvie Freemason
Cameron, Donald	Gardener & Piper c 1900
Campbell, Ivy (Mr)	Banker, 3rd Treasurer BWC to 1889
Campbell, John	'Red Block': Colporteur c 1900
Cant, Robert	'Benard', took over Robertson's shop c1900
Carrick, David	Tinsmith, Director Buch. Water Co.
Carrick, John	Blacksmith:Chair of Buch.Wat.Co
Carrick, Miss	Rockhill: Last of the Carricks c1900
Christie, Jane	Grocers/Shopkeepers in 1860
Clark, Sam	Rail Station Blacksmith c 1900
Clelland, Rev John	1st Minister, North Church 1752
Cowan, Alexander	Carrick Buildings c1900
Cowie, John	Taylor Place c 1900
MacRae's	Alpine Bakery & Tearoom 1930s
Mack, David	Village Bank Manager & Freeason
Marshall, Dr	East end of the village
Matson, James	Farmer 'The Thirds' c 1900

McAdam, Mrs	Tenant Rob Roy Htl c1900
Cowie, Miss Kate	North Manse, schoolteacher
Cowie, Rev G.W.S	Sec. Village Hall C/Tee 1919–31
	United Free Manse:Last Chr of BWComp
Crawford, Brigadier	Chair: Village Hall C/Tee 1946–9, 1950–8
Crawford, Colonel	Auchentroig
Currie, Charles	Joiner c1900
Dalgleish, George	Schoolmaster: 2nd Treas.Buc.Wat.Cot to 1887
Davidson, James	Pig Dealer:Director Buch Water Co
Dick, James	Emigrated to USA in 1907
Dolan, Hugh	Drainer c1900
Donaldson, Peter	Wagonman for MacPhie's, Grocers c1900
Douglas, Mr	Gartmore Estate Agent c1870
Dow, George	Village Constable & Freemason
Drysdale, Henry	Main St: Saddler/'Dentist' c1900
Duff, G	General Merchant & Freemason
Duff, The Misses	'Alpine House': Main St c 1900
Duncan, Keir	Cattle dealer in 1860
Dun, Alexander	Farmer 'Craignaughton' c 1900
	Married Margaret Risk
	Farmer & Director Buch Water Co
Dun, Andrew	Baker's vanman/Roadman
Dun, Andrew (1802–76)	Married Elizabeth Strang: father of Alex
Dun, Annie (d.1949)	Married Morrison, Blacksmith in 1903
Dun, Rev A. (1718–90)	Minister of Cadder, father of Alexander
Edwards, Jean	Main Street, c1900
Finlayson, John	Dairyman, Mye Road
Fisher, Daniel	Balamenoch: 4th Chr of Buch.Wat.Co to 1910
Fisher, Donald	Chair: Village Hall C/Tee 1949–50
Fisher, Daniel Jr.	6th Chr of Buch.Wat.Co to 1926
Fisher, Mr	Chair: Village Hall C/Tee 1886–1928
Fleming, John	Farmer ' Lower Ballaird ' c 1900
Fleming, John M.	Killed in World War 1
Flemming, William	Farmer(Lr Ballaird) & Freemason
Forrester in Ballochneck	Manager to build North Church
Galbraith, John	Miller in 1860
Galbraith, Walter	'Benview': Solicitor in Glasgow c 1900
Gardiner, A & J	Farmers ' Gartentreuch' c 1900
George, Miss Annie	Took over the McAlpine Shoe Business
Gibb, J.B.	Stationmaster in 1903
Gorrie, Charlie	Signal Fitter at the Station c 1900
Graham, John	Butcher & Director Buch.Water Co.
Graham, RB Cunninghame	Laird at Gartmore c1870
Haddow, John	Farmer 'Easter Kepdowrie' c 1900
Hain, John	Licensee Station Hotel c1900
Hall, J.G.	Sec. Village Hall C/Yee 1931–8, 1944–57
Harper, Mr	'Springbank':Exciseman
Harvey, David	Wheelwright in 1860
Harvey, John	Farmer 'The Heights' c 1900
Harvie, David	Joiner: 3rd Chair Of Buch. Wat. Co to 1885
Harvie, James	Joiner c1900
Hay, Peter	Parish Clerk:1st Master of the Freemasons
Hendry, Mr J	Tailor: Taylor Place shop c 1900
John Risk, Weaver	Manager to build North Church
Kay, Jane	Vintner in 1860
Keir, Duncan	Publican, 1st Treasurer Buch. Water Co.
Keir, Mrs Lilly	Licensee of The Buchlyvie Hotel c1900
Kennedy, Dan	Wood merchant and curler c 1900
Kidd, John	Boot & Shoemaker in 1860
Laing, Duggald	Chaffeur (Ballamenoch) & Freemason
Lennie of Gartinstarry	Manager to build North Church
Liddle, The Misses	'Benview' c 1900
Lindsay, Mrs	Doctor's wife, Dunstan House
Lindsay, R.W.	'Springbank',Station Rd:Doctor for 40+ yrs
Liston, William	Marine Engineer & Freemason

Livingstone, James	Carrier in 1860
MacDonald, Rev. John	Minister, East (South) Church, 1903
	Sec. Village Hall C/Tee1885–1915
McAllister, Alex	Boot & Shoemaker in 1860
McAlpine, Duncan	Shoemaker
McAlpine, John	Boot & Shoemaker in 1860
McAlpine, Peter	Draper, Chrmn Buch Water Comittee c1870
McArthur, James	Joiner & Cartwright 1930s
McCaig, Malcolm	Motor engineer/ Petrol Staion/Garage
McCallum, Miss Bella	Confectioners c 1900
McCallum, Mrs	Red Lion Licensee, 1903
McDowall, William	Chauffeur (Buchlyvie Lodge) & Freemason
McEwan, John	Railway surfaceman
McEwan, John	Grocers/Shopkeepers in 1860
McEwan, Miss Margaret	Postmistress c1900
McEwan, Tom	5th Sec/Treas. to 1918
McEwans	Tom, Andrew and John: 'Spittalton' c1900
McEwen, John	Vintner in 1860
McFarlane, Alexander	Tailor in 1860
McFarlane, Duncan	Coachman: Director Buch Water Co.
McFarlane, George	Station Master, 1st Secretary Buch Water
McFarlane, James	Farmer ' Oxhill' c 1900
McFarlane, Peter	Village lamplighter c 1900/Postman
McFarlane, Robert	Milk delivery in the 1930s
McFarlane, Walter	Grocer
McGregor, W	Signalman at the Station c 1900
McGregor, William	Tailor in 1860
McIntyre, Mrs	Carrick Buildings c1900
McIntyre, Peter	Saddler & Freemason
McIntyre, Robert	'Howe Cottage': Rtrd gamekeeper c1900
McIntyre, Robert	Contractor & Innkeeper
McKechnie, Miss Jesse	Village Hall cleaner/caretaker c 1900
McKeich, William	Farmer/Woodend: Bred Baron of Buchlyvie
McKellar, Mr	Tenant of Cashley & Gowstone Farm c1870
McKerracher, John	Farmer 'Easter Mye' c 1900
McLaughlan, John	Grocers/Shopkeepers in 1860
McLellan, Dan	Whiteley's Farm Rd c 1900
McLellan, James	Burn Green: Contractor/Footballer c1900
McLuckie, Robert	Farmer:1st Chair. Buch. Water Co to 1870
McMaster, Mrs	Springbank:Grand–daughter of James McPhie
McNab, Frances	Taylor Place c 1900
McOnie, John	Glenside: 5th Chair of Buch.Wat.Co to 1918
McOnie, Robert	Draper/Farmer:Director Buc Water Co.
McOnie, Robert	Farmer ' Higher Culbowie' c 1900
McOnie, Thomas	Farmer 'Lower Culbowie' c 1900
McPhail, Archie	Village Constable c 1900
McPhie, Alexander	'Springbank'
McPhie, Billy	Son of emigrants. Hudson Bay Co after 1900
McPhie, James	Boot & Shoemaker in 1860
McPhie, James	Grocer & Grain Merchant: Director BWC
McPhie, James Jr	His widow & children to Canada c 1900
McPhie, James Snr	Shoemaker & Boot salesman
McPhie, Miss Mary	Draper: Main Street c1900
McQueen, Miss Sally	Culbowie Farm Rd c 1900
McQuisten	Maggie and Christina, daughters of Joe
McQuisten, Joe	Main Street: c 1900
McQuisten, Robert	Son of Joe: Killed in a van accident
McQuisten, William	Son of Joe: Veterinerian c 1900
McVean, Dougal & Katie	Station Rd c 1900
Meek, John	Farmer 'Wester Mye' c 1900
Melrose, Miss	Rosebank, Music Teacher/Organist
Miller, John	Grocer in the 1930s
Milne, John	Bank Teller c 1900
Montgomery, John	Painter/local singer/Freemason
Moore, Robert	Farmer 'Mains c 1900

Morris, The Rev Alex.	Minister of Free Church c1870
Morrison Feuar of Buch.	Manager to build North Church
Morrison, Jean	Related to Robert McLuckie
Morrison, John	Blacksmith, succeeded Archie Weir
Morrison, John	Manager:Village Co–op branch: Freemason
Morrison, Peggy (d.1986)	married John Smith of Garden in 1930
Morrison, Roderick	Tailor c1900
Mortimer Rev G.R.	Sec. Village Hall C/Yee 1938–44
Napier, Andrew	Killed in the Boer War
Napier, Miss Agnes	Whiteley's Farm Rd c 1900
Neilson, Helen	Grocers/Shopkeepers in 1860
Neish, John	Hawked Fish (AW) c1900
Parlane, John	Farmer 'Easter Offerance' c 1900
Parlane, Katie	Carrick Buildings c1900
Parlane, Walter	Feuar & Farmer
Parlane, William	Farmer ' Wester Offerance' c 1900
Paterson, Tom	Tailor c 1900
Ramsay, Alexander	Saddler in 1860
Ramsay, Mrs	Laundry c 1900
Reoch, James	of Gartenstarry: Owned 1st Village Car
Richardson, William	Master Baker/ 2nd Freemason–Master 1922
Risk, James	Farmer 'Gowstone' c 1900
Risk, Mrs	Pend Close: Kept a parrot(AW) c1900
Risk, Robert	Maltster in 1860
Robertson, James	Signalman at the Station c 1900
Rose, Rev Mr	'Dunstan': Minister:Free Church c 1900
Service, The Misses	'Broomfield' c 1900
Shearer, Andrew	Master Tailor & Freemason
Shearer, Hugh	Tailor in c1900
Smith, Bob	Linesman for the railway c 1900
Smith, Jeanie	Married Alexander Buchanan in 1954
Smith, Mrs Peggy	Related to Robert McLuckie
Spittal, John	Insurance Inspector & Freemason
Steel, David	Farmer 'Higher Ballaird' c 1900
Steel, John	Butcher c 1900
Stewart, Alex	Farmer 'Blairgorts' c 1900
Stewart, Alexander	Millwright
Stewart, Alexander	Wheelwright in 1860
Stewart, Andrew	'Harperstane Cottage': Gardener
Stewart, Bob	'Bank Cottage c1900
Stewart, James	Farmer 'Cashley' c 1900
Stewart, James	Cashley Farm: Director of Buch Water Co.
Stewart, James G	Plumber & Footballer(Alloa & St.J's) 1903
Stewart, John	'Harperstane': Killed on the railway
Stewart, Robert	Farmer ' Balwill' c 1900
Stewart, William	Boot & Shoemaker in 1860
Stirling, Col	Chair: Village Hall C/Tee 1928–46
Stirling, James	Lord Lieutenant of Stirlingshire
Stirling, John	Master of Garden in 1724
Stranf, James	Farmer ' Knockinshannoch' c 1900
Taylor, Bob	Cottage (Replaced by Drs.Surgery)c1900
Taylor, Miss Jean	Taylor Place c 1900
Turnbull, Miss	Farmer 'Badenkep c 1900
Watt, Rev. John	Minister (East Church) & Freemason
Webster, Robert	Killed in the Boer War
Weir, Alexander	Last Treasurer/Secretary BWC to 1932
	Freemason of 1st Buchlyvie Lodge
Weir, Archibald	Blacksmith:Director Buch Water Co.
Weir, James	Village:Blacksmith & Farmer at Whiteleys
Whyte, Charles	LNER & Musical Director of BADOS
Wilkie, Mr	Mye Farm
Wilson, James	Baker in 1860
Wilson, William	Hall Cottage: Mole Trapper c1900
Wood, Mr	'Rockhill' c 1900
Zuill, Family	Station Rd c 1900

Bibliography

Anderson, The Rev W Second Statistical Account of the Parish of Kippen 1841

Cooper, J P "The Fall of the Stuart Monarchy" Ch 18 New Cambridge Modern Hist. Vol 4 1970

Corbett, Dix et al. Central Scotland:Land, Wildlife, People: Forth Naturalist & Historian 1993

Buchanan's Guide to Strathendrick, Aberfoyle & District 1902

De Beer E.S   The English Revolution: Chpt 6 from New Cambridge Modern History 1960

Devine, T. M. Exploring the Scottish Past: Tuckwell Press 1995

Dicks, T R B The Stirling Region, Chapter 10. Stirling University

P.Dun Summer at the Lake of Menteith: 1867: Oliver & Boyd, Edinburgh

George, T Neville "The Stirling Region "Chpt. 1 and 2: Stirling Univ.1974

Graeme, Louisa G. Or and Sable, a Book of the Graemes and Grahams: William Brown, Edinburgh 1903

Mackie J.D. A History of Scotland: Penguin Books 1966

MacFarlane, Walter Geographical Collections edited Mitchell in Scot. Hist. Soc 1906

MacKay, K J H "On first looking into Chapman's Ledger "Forth Naturalist and Historian Vol I 1976

Main, Lorna Excavations at the Fairy Knowe, Buchlyvie 1975–78. Forth Naturalist and Historian Vol 3 1978

Martin, T "The Stirling Region "Chapter 9. Stirling Univ. 1974

Mitchell Rev JC 3rd Statitical account of the Parish of Kippen (1966) Chapter 15

Muirhead, David Notes on the Agricultural Associations of Buchlyvie 1996

Parker. T M Protestantism and confessional strife "New Cambridge Modern History Vol 3 1968

Registerum Magni The Register of the Great Seal of Scotland: Regum Scotorum Edited by Paul & Thomson
        (1513–46): The Scot. Record Soc.: Clark Constable 1984

Russell & Cowie Bi–Centenary of Buchlyvie North Church 1902. Kennedy & Christie

Smith, John G. Strathendrick and its Inhabitants from early times 1896

Smout T.C. A History of the Scottish People 1530–1830: Collins/Fontana 1972

Smout T.C. A Century of the Scottish People: 1830–1950: Fontana Press 1987

Stirling D.C. Development & Planning Dept: Focus 1991 Census: Stirling District/Buchlyvie

Summers, Gilbert J Rob Roy MacGregor: Jarrold Publishing 1995

Timms, Duncan "The Stirling Region." Stirling Univ. 1974

Thomas, John Forgotten Railways: Scotland 2nd Edition 1981 David & Charles

Weir, Alexander The Village Fifty Years Ago: Stirling Observer 1953, 1954, 1956, 1962, 1965. (Mrs Jessie
        Ritchie).